MY PEOPLE

A HISTORY OF THE NATIVE AMERICANS

KA-BE-MUB-BE / WILLIAM CAMUS – FLEURUS

© of the american edition :

Editions Fleurus, Paris, 1997

ISBN : 0-7651-9104-0

© Editions Fleurus, Paris, 1995 for the original edition.
Title of the French edition :
Ainsi vivaient mes ancêtres les Indiens.
English translation by Translate-A-Book,
a division of Transedition Limited, Oxford, England
Printed in France
Distributor in the USA : SMITHMARK Publishers Inc
115 west 18th street, New York, NY 10011
Distributor in Canada : PROLOGUE Inc
1650 Bd Lionel Bertrand, Boisbriand, Québec J7H4N7

Ka-Be-Mub-Be

Ka-Be-Mub-Be was born in 1923 in the Yukon province of Canada. His father, a full-blooded Iroquois, married a French-Canadian woman. Ka-Be-Mub-Be grew up among elk, wolves, moose, bears, and huskies. His playmate was a bear cub, from which he had to be parted when it grew to more than 600 pounds. At the age of nine, the child even became the leader of a pack of wolves! His father taught him to set traps, to hunt, and to fish in the icy northern waters. But traveling across the vast snow-covered plains of the north with his dogs was the thing that Ka-Be-Mub-Be preferred above all else. In this way the young Indian's life went on peacefully, until the day when his mother Émilienne decided to introduce him to "civilization".... Ka-Be-Mub-Be was just eleven years old.

He lived for seven long years in France, where he took the name William Camus. But the longing for freedom, which never left him, prompted him to return to America. After his studies at Laval University in Montreal, Quebec, he became a professional stock-car driver in Indianapolis, and then an international reporter. He campaigned for his Native American comrades through the American Indian Movement (AIM), and took part in meetings of the National Congress of American Indians (NCAI). Finally, he returned to France, where he became a writer.

At the age of sixty-nine he declared that he could no longer live without his friends from the old days, so his wife traveled to the north of Canada and brought him back a splendid wolf with blue eyes. With him, William Camus set out once more for the lands of his Indian ancestors, from which he brought back pieces of ancient legends garnered from Indian elders in Canada, the United States and Mexico.

To date, William Camus has written more than fifty books.

He has recently been awarded, in Madrid, the "Barco del Vapor" prize for his book *The Rain Maker*, which has sold more than 100,000 copies.

Ka-Be-Mub-Be/William Camus is considered to be an important historian of American Indians. He still speaks his native language, along with five or six others. At seventy-two years of age, he is a stranger to illness; like his dog Hus-Ky, he is rarely tired! In this book, this modern Iroquois reveals to us stories of his Indian ancestors.

Foreword

One day, to remind me of the order of things, the Great Spirit said to me: "You are an Indian, write as an Indian."

Many non-native historians have written about the Indians, but, I hope they will forgive me for saying that, no matter how erudite they may be, most of them have not truly understood the events or the ideas they were describing, because they were interpreting things by reasoning as Wa-Sic-Hus, or "Man-Mind" in Dakota (a nickname given to the white missionaries). There is a world of difference between what a non-native and an Indian can feel when faced with the same situation.

It would be futile to speak here of all the native peoples of America as there are an enormous variety of Indian customs and ways. A tribe living on the snow-covered plains regarded the sun as a benevolent god; another, residing on the edge of a stifling desert, saw a malevolent god who burned and dried out everything. The Indian peoples spoke more than 300 languages, and their philosophy and customs differed from one nation to another. There are at least as many differences between a Canadian Iroquois and a Mexican Apache as between a person from Sweden and one from Portugal!

No one knows for certain the origins of the Native Americans. Scholars generally believe that they migrated from Asia across the then-frozen Bering Sea about 70,000 years ago. Many Indian mythologies point to an origin below the earth. Where exactly did these untiring wanderers come from? I will therefore avoid trying to untangle this web. It seems to me pointless to put forward theories about a problem that is, after all, of little interest to many Indians. Some call this being cautious; I say, not cautious, but wise!

Paleface, you will turn this page and read. You will
find yourself gaping with astonishment: therefore
take great care to put your hand over your mouth,
so that your spirit does not fly away, never to
return.

The Indian as the Great Spirit made him

The basic ideas of the Indian, whatever his tribe, manifested numerous similarities. He placed great importance on politeness and propriety. Each individual could act freely within the limits of custom. If languages differed from one group to another, Indians communicated with their hands, their behavior, smoke… and all the items the Great Spirit had given to them.

Wa-kan-da (one name for Great Spirit) had created nature and it was nature that inspired the Indian. Contemplative by nature, she spent time meditating and drawing tranquility and wisdom from the vastness and intimate detail of creation.

Indian Courtesy

"**M**y brother seems hungry. Has he not eaten?" When receiving a visitor, Indian hospitality always begins in this way. While many non-natives may be overly concerned about their health, Indians believe that on a full stomach one forgets one's cares. The Indian traditionally gave such importance to propriety that she never asked, "Where have you been?" or "What have you done?" For her, direct questions are the height of bad manners. But, curious as an old owl, through convoluted means and after a long conversation, she will still obtain the answer she seeks. Non-natives who were unaware of these customs complained that they could never get a straight answer and were astonished that the Indians seemed unhappy about the slightest direct question put to them. In truth, they would sadly consider just how rude "civilized" people could be!

The Indian vocabulary contained no swear words. To say that someone is of bad origins is highly offensive. The offended person withdraws into a corner until the one who insulted him comes to apologize and offer him presents. Obviously, the more expensive these are, the quicker the apologies are accepted.

Eager to show bravery and holding themselves to a strict code of honor, Indians can be very proud of themselves. They shout their own praises at the top of their voices, or are full of shame and hide themselves away.

Courtesy occasionally demanded that an enemy, met by chance, should become a temporary brother. In such cases, warriors put down their weapons, brought out the peace pipe, and smoked together.

CHOUARD DE GROSEILLER

In 1716, Médard Chouard de Groseiller had the opportunity to witness an encounter between Comanches and Dakotas. This trapper, or coureur de bois, as they were called at the time, traded with a band of Dakotas whose chief was called Blind Mole. Every year, Médard Chouard de Groseiller bartered for skins with the Dakotas. Blind Mole viewed him as a friend, so much so that one day he asked him to take part in an attack on his enemies, the Comanches. He claimed to have read in the "signs" that he would be victorious if a non-native fought on his side. To avoid angering the great chief, Médard accepted, but determined to stay out of the fray. This is what he related to a priest about the battle: "We had been riding for two days when we came across a fifty-strong band of Comanches. The Dakotas numbered around forty. Blind Mole immediately decided to attack, but hardly had the battle commenced when the sky turned black with clouds and a storm began. In the rain, Blind Mole stopped fighting,

and I was amazed to hear him say to the enemy chief, who was called Ee-sha-ko-nee, Bow-and-Shield, 'Brave warrior, see all this water falling from the sky, see our lovely clothes, our most beautiful war costumes: the rain is spoiling them and making them dull. See also, oh Ee-sha-ko-nee, the mud which covers the battlefield. Our Braves cannot die in a swamp. This is not a good day to die!' Bow-and-Shield reflected on this and replied, 'My heart has heard you and my mouth says yes! You have seen well, and know that your wisdom is so great that now the Comanches name you Blind-Mole-who-Sees-Clearly. I have spoken and it is good. Waho!' "The two bands separated, and on the way home I saw the Dakota braves look on Blind Mole with envy, because he had done a noble deed. Back at the camp, the chief explained to me that it took the women more than one snow to make a war costume, and that it would be stupid to ruin them for a battle which could be continued in better weather. I subsequently learned that certain enemy tribes had an agreed sign when they encountered each other in the winter and the ground was covered in snow. This sign meant, 'It's too cold, we will fight in the Season of Good Weather.' By common agreement, they went on their way."

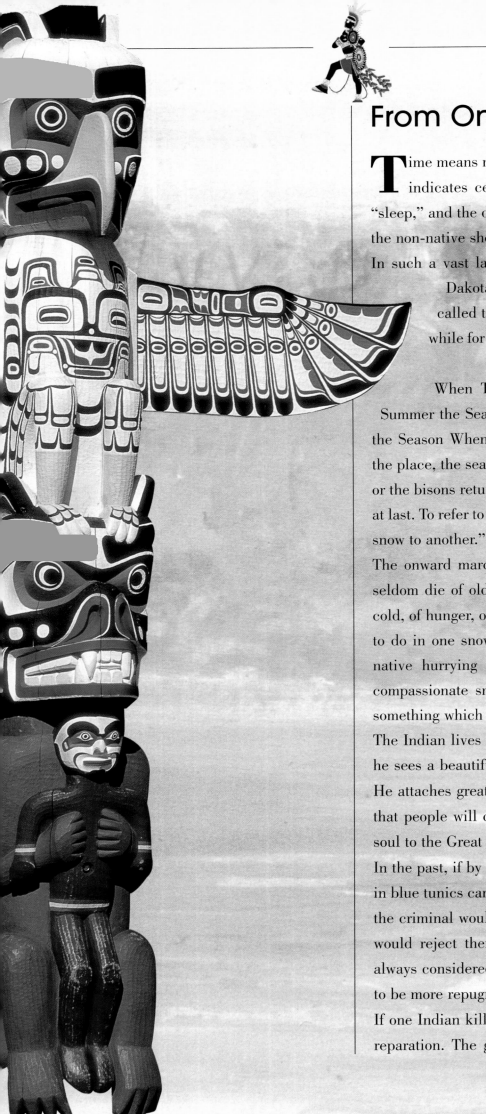

From One Sun to Another

Time means nothing to the Native, except that the path of the sun indicates certain phases of the day. Between days there is a "sleep," and the day is a "sun." When an Indian speaks of a "moon," the non-native should understand a month.

In such a vast land, the seasons vary from north to south. For the Dakota who live in Montana, the depths of winter are called the Season When The Snow Comes Into The Tepees, while for the Southern Apaches this period becomes the Time Of Gentle Days, and the Spring is called the Season When The Female Bison Gives Birth. An Iroquois calls Summer the Season When The Cherries are Red, and the Autumn, the Season When The Stags Lose Their Horns. Thus, depending on the place, the seasons are the times when Indians can collect berries, or the bisons return to the plain in large numbers, or the maize is ripe at last. To refer to a complete year, the northern Indian says, "from one snow to another."

The onward march of time doesn't mean very much to people who seldom die of old age in their beds, but more often of sunstroke, of cold, of hunger, or of a bullet from warfare. What an Indian is unable to do in one snow, he does in another snow. When she sees a non-native hurrying to finish a task, the Indian simply says with a compassionate smile, "The Paleface is crazy to hurry so much for something which he could equally well do tomorrow."

The Indian lives with a keen awareness of his eventual death. When he sees a beautiful sunny morning, he says, "It's a good day to die." He attaches great importance to his death, because it is through this that people will continue to speak of him when he has given up his soul to the Great Spirit.

In the past, if by chance an Indian killed a white person, the soldiers in blue tunics came into the tribe to seize the killer. To make amends, the criminal would offer them gifts in compensation, but the soldiers would reject them and lead him away to be hanged. The Indians always considered the sight of a person hanging on the end of a rope to be more repugnant than the crime he may have committed.

If one Indian killed another, the dead person's family would demand reparation. The guilty party would offer presents, and the incident would likely be settled. If he could not afford this expense, he went into exile in shame, was driven away by his family for breaking the rules of propriety, or was occasionally killed in retribution. The Indians did not acknowledge the right of non-natives to summarily condemn one of their own people to death.

This way of seeing things created a barrier between the two races. The words "bravery" and "cowardice" did not have the same meaning. For Indians, the greatest courage might lay in fleeing from an enemy when outnumbered. Unlike Westerners, Indians could begin a battle and stop it a minute later for practical reasons. The Indian philosophy allowed them to engage in behavior that was inconceivable to non-natives.

Although Indians love colorful legends and wide open spaces, their artistic sense coexists quite nicely with a strong impulse toward practicality. The green prairie is lovely in her eyes if it fattens the bison on which her people depend for food. A beautiful forest could be seen as a store of dead or half-charred wood that she can collect easily to warm herself. A row of elk haunches makes an unrivaled decoration for the entrance to her tepee. The non-native settler's wooden barrel can become the most marvelous of objects: from its metal hoops an Indian can fashion the points of his arrows and the tips of his lances so that he can hunt more effectively. The Native is a pragmatist, and for him, a bird in the hand is worth two in the bush!

THUNDERBIRD

The warrior, Thunderbird, owed his name to a dream. An eagle, holding a thunderbolt in his claws, appeared to him in a dream he had in the sweatlodge. Believing that this vision told him that he was a descendant of the Great Spirit, who had chosen him to be an extraordinary being, he informed his fellows that he had become an invulnerable warrior. Once each year, between battles, Thunderbird went to the top of a mountain, to a place called the pipe quarry, to visit his powerful "relation." When he came back he had super-natural gifts and extremely useful qualities for fighting his tribe's enemies, who believed him to be immortal.

Freedom of Thought

The Native Americans' freedom of thought and action bothered Euro-Americans. The Indian could behave without risk of criticism from his fellows, so long as his conduct did not bring his honor or the good name of his nation into disrepute. This freedom sometimes led to excess. Indian morality could appear radically different from that of non-natives. For instance, when, around the age of puberty, if a young Dakota Indian did not feel any desire for bloodshed, he gave up his status as a man. At a tribal council, he stated his wish to become a Hee-ma-neh. Then, the members of the tribe organized a great feast, at which the women gave him an embroidered dress, bearing symbols that indicated his new identity. By currying favor with an unmarried man or a widower, a Hee-ma-neh was able to enter a tepee, and, with the permission of the owner, to make it his home. There, he took on the tasks traditionally undertaken by a woman. The Hee-ma-neh was not looked down on by the members of the tribe. When he passed by, the men did not put their hands over their mouths: to make fun of him or to insult him would be to bring dishonor on themselves. Among the Iroquois, many of these "bardaches" became famous. They could sit among the council of elders and were listened to by the most distinguished warriors.

Indian Names

Among many non-natives, an old dictum states, "Tell me your name and I will tell you who you are!" However, people change throughout their lives. Whereas non-natives do not significantly change their names, Indians….

Among many Indians, a child never bears the name of his parents. She is given a name at birth, but it is a designation that is not used, and that guards her soul. This name remains a secret, and to ask what it is would be an affront, lacking the most basic manners. To divulge it would mean casting her soul to the winds, earning the disdain and contempt of her companions. She would quickly be nicknamed, "She Who No Longer Has A Name," and her only option would be to leave the tribe until she was able to accomplish an act of generosity or bravery that would earn her a new name. For the child, things are not so simple. The fact that her name is a secret means her mother must give her another. This one is not chosen, but dictated by an event, which may be quite trivial. The child could be called Sitting Toad without any injury to her young dignity. Her mother could call her this simply because she saw such a toad when she was giving birth. This child could equally well be called Noise Of A Fire Stick, if at her birth a gunshot was heard not far away.

An Indian changes names several times in the course of his life. Depending on the tribe, these changes are decided by the elders, or more simply by one's family or companions. Sometimes the individual is consulted and can reject the new name if he feels it will cast a shadow on his health, his abilities, or his medicine. Sometimes he has no say in the matter and the change is made whether he likes it or not. If he wants to communicate his dissatisfaction, he might ask for someone to whisper his new name three times into his ear. Then he twists and turns, as if he were in pain, so that the others may realize that this name makes him ill, that it is bad medicine, and that it is totally unsuitable for him.

Euro-Americans tend to scorn Indian names. But things that carry meaning for the Indian do not necessarily do so for non-natives. The two peoples have such different views about many things that it seems reasonable to admit that the latter may be mistaken.

THOSE WHO MAKE THE STONES BOIL

In 1840, the painter George Caitlin wrote down in his travel journals the names of the Indians he encountered. Among others, he speaks of the Assiniboins, Those Who Make The Stones Boil, whose chief was called Wi-jun-jon, Head Like a Pigeon's Egg, and his wife, Chin-cha-pee, Gliding Fire Insect. It was the Ojibwas who gave the Assiniboins their name. They saw them heating stones before throwing them into holes filled with water to cook their food, and named them Those Who Make the Stones Boil; but the Indians, of course, did not actually make stones boil. The more exact version would be Those Who Heat The Stones.

Concerning the name Gliding Fire Insect, it is again without doubt due to a misinterpretation, as the Assiniboin vocabulary does not contain a word for insect. Logic requires that this woman's name was Gliding Fire Bird. The Fire Bird was the vengeful god of this tribe. Chin-cha-pee may have seen a gliding eagle in the sky and adopted this magical name. But it's risky to try to interpret other cultures with little knowledge of those cultures. Regarding Head Like a Pigeon's Egg, the whites thought that this man was afflicted with a deformed skull, but this was not the case. So, did his name refer to his lack of intelligence? Absolutely not! Win-jun-jon became a great shaman and had to be sent into exile by his people because his medicine aroused so much fear for their future. He finally fell victim to alcoholism and disappeared around 1874.

Most Indian names remain largely incomprehensible to non-natives. However, some names do not seem so mysterious. A crippled old woman, worn out by hard work, was called O'Rulh, Nothing. An alert, fresh-faced young woman was called Pure Leaping Fountain.

Indian Languages

The numerous and varied Indian languages cannot easily be translated because there are no word-for-word equivalents. Instead, it is necessary to think like an Indian, to see things through her eyes, to know the event that gave rise to the name. Even so, it is still possible to be mistaken. For a Crow Indian called Sha-ee-shopes, which means Four Wolves, a non-native will imagine a great warrior flying into battle, his hair standing on end, clawing to the right, biting to the left, unleashed like four wolves.

In fact, his friends may have called him Sha-ee-shopes because one day four wolves barred his way and he ran like a coward. For the non-native, the Indian name remains mysterious and full of pitfalls, all the more because the Indians often change their names. A person's bearing can give rise to one name, a change of behavior can call for another. It is one's day-to-day actions, one's behavior in the hunt or in battle, and external natural or supernatural events that suggest Native American names.

The Indian called He Who Sees Things In His Head could be the worst of liars or a holy man. One who bears the name Wild Horse could be a highly strung, bad-tempered and threatening figure, or may quite simply have been bitten by a wild horse. The Man Who Walks In His Shadow may be thrifty or an idler who spends the day in the shade of his wigwam. A young Indian called Who Does Not Hunt, on returning from his first hunt with three kills pierced by three arrows bearing his symbol, will become Three Arrows. On another occasion, returning with four kills, he will see himself named Four Arrows. Then he may stumble on a stone and slip into the river in front of witnesses, and he may become Wet Moccasins.

These different names might be adopted if the incidents that gave rise to them had been sufficiently noted by the elders. If the elders consider that the name is a slur on the honor of the individual, they can change it and call the person She Who is Not Talked About. Then all is for the best and everyone is happy.

SITTING BULL –
THE GREAT DAKOTA SORCERER

We know that the early New World colonists were not all English, and many spoke that language very badly. Understandably, these people understood the Hunkpapa language even less. This is probably the source of the mistake in the translation of the name of the great sorcerer Sitting Bull, although the image is nonetheless a good reflection of his character. One could imagine this leader seated, as powerful as a bison, his head crowned with two horns. The most widespread version of the story states that Sitting Bull was an extremely courageous hunter. He would not hesitate to jump from his horse onto the back of a bison to plunge his long knife straight into the animal's heart. The first time his brothers saw him act in this way, according to the legend, they called him He Who Sat On The Bison, which had quite a different meaning than Sitting Bull. One may look at his symbol, which can be seen on the rare documents that he signed with the United States. The drawing shows a riderless bison. The horns that appear on the head of the signatory leave no room for doubt about the rank he occupies in the tribe. In effect, this Dakota had the right to the title of "bison," that is, he could wear the ceremonial two-horned bonnet.

Historians sometimes overlook the obvious in their haste to over-complicate or to simplify. We would still be left writing postscripts on Sitting Bull's name if an old Indian in Montana had not offered me a more prosaic explanation: before adopting the name Sitting Bull, the Hunkpapa shaman had been called Ta-na-ho-ka-te, Leaper of Rapids, by his people, because of his great agility. Alas, with advancing age, he developed rheumatism! At the end of his life, his legs had difficulty in carrying his weight, and the old bison never missed the slightest excuse to sit down.

The Hunkpapa sorcerer, Leaper of Rapids, was in his day called Leaping Squirrel by a white man who apparently did not understand all the subtleties of the Indian languages.

CLOTHES THAT SPEAK

Like most people, Indians were able to express themselves in many ways. They would, for instance, use an animal skin cloak. If an elder had an important decision to make, he arranged his garment on his shoulders in a particular way. If a man wanted to invite another to go hunting, the folds of his cloak announced that he knew a good place. The different ways of wrapping oneself in one's cloak could signify, "I'm going to the council" or "Don't speak to me, I need to think."

Signs and Messages

Myself

Look ahead

The exact number of language and dialects spoken by American Indians has never been well established. In the 1700s, at least three hundred different dialects may have been in common use. With so many different forms of speech, groups often had a hard time understanding one another.

Two Apache groups living fifty miles from each other might encounter difficulties in understanding each other. It was the same for the Dakota, Iroquois, or Utes, who nevertheless had to communicate in order to mark out territorial boundaries, to divide hunting grounds, to trade, and to conclude all sorts of agreements.

In general, however, Indians communicated very well among themselves. When speech became impossible they used various forms of sign language.

Do many people know that they are speaking a universal language when they brush the palm of their hand over the forehead to say, "I've had it up to here," or when they raise a fatalistic arm over the shoulder to signify, "We'll find out tomorrow," or again, when they pass the edge of a hand beneath the chin while thinking, "I'll cut his throat."

There are so many gestures that people use instinctively without knowing where they come from. A language of gestures was brought to Europe in the 18th century by American trappers. These men often used sign language when trading with Indians. On returning to their own countries, they retained these gestures and

One person

A white person

On horseback

The language of signs

popularized their use.

Anyone who has not seen two Indians having a discussion in sign language cannot imagine the colorfulness of the conversation. Deaf people have an analogous language, but the Indian phrases are shorter and more rapid. In the style of semaphore, she executed broad movements with her arms. Her gestures were imbued with both grace and logic. To say, "I have eaten well," she would strike her chest with her fist, then put two fingers into her mouth and trace circles on her stomach. If, in addition, she made a gesture indicating that her stomach was bulging, the sense of the phrase changed to mean, "I've eaten a lot." This means of communication allowed the introduction of the nuances and fine distinctions of language.

Many Indian words for their own people may be translated simply as "people." Some Indians referred to themselves by raising the left index finger. For non-natives, they traced a horizontal line across the forehead to refer to the hat that whites often wore jammed tightly on their heads. If by chance an Indian wished to specify that a non-native was on horseback, two of his fingers were placed astride the palm of the other hand. Certain gestures made at the beginning of the phrase indicated the past, the future, the present, the conditional, or the question form. As a "speaker" moved his arms, the fringes of his sleeves would twirl as he signed the rivers, the mountains, the sun, the stars, ... or himself!

The entire life story of the Mandan chief Ma-to-toh-pah is summarized on his bison-skin cloak.

Smoke Signals

Indians could communicate among themselves by "reading" the smoke that rose to the sky. With the help of puffs of smoke, it was possible to send a message over long distances, as far as the eye could see.

To send his information, the Indian from a culture that used smoke signals chose a high spot in an open place and lit a bright fire. Two of his companions took charge of a blanket, and a third held bunches of lush grass. On a signal from He Who Holds The Secret Of The Symbols, the grass was thrown onto the fire and white smoke rose up straight into the skies. This signal meant: message begins. Then, on the instructions of He Who Holds The Secret Of The Symbols, the assistants covered up the fire for a moment and then uncovered it quickly. White "balls" of various sizes rose into the sky, separated by pauses of varying lengths. The one who fed the fire made sure that the smoke was always thick and consistent, and the slow dance continued. These signs cannot be likened to Morse Code, which consists of only dots and dashes. In fact, smoke signals were more subtle: the size of each puff of smoke, the length of the pause, as well as the color of the smoke given off had a precise meaning. White smoke signified victory,

Only the initiated knew how to interpret smoke signals. A black wisp of smoke announced a death; one white puff followed by two black ones meant, "we attack"; two round puffs interspersed with straight wisps indicated, "we are bringing home two dead." Thus, the joys and sorrows of a people were communicated from one village to another.

feasting, and good medicine. Among the Dakota, black smoke signified sorrow, defeat, and bad medicine. According to the plants used, the smoke took on a black or white hue and plunged the receivers into the deepest despair or the greatest happiness.

Although all Indians of certain tribes knew how to interpret the puffs of smoke, the art of creating them was the privilege of a few initiates.

Waysigns

Native Americans could also transmit information by using waysigns, which were more discreet than smoke signals. When a column was on the move, an advance party prepared the way and kept the leaders informed not only about what they would encounter on the path, but also about the things they could not see to either side of the convoy. Such messages were left by the scouts.

They were put together from whatever people found on the way: twigs and branches if the column was passing through a forest, tufts of grass on the plain, and pebbles in the stony deserts. If by ill luck none of these materials was available, Indians traced the explanatory sketches in the sand. A hungry and thirsty non-native could pass over and over again along that path without noticing that 1,000 feet away a river flowed, behind a low hill that also hid a herd of bison.

The leader of the column would constantly look at the ground and recognize the often minuscule signs, which told him, "A bowshot away on the left, there is water," "We are hunting three bisons," "Beware, enemy warriors in sight," "Halt! Soldiers across the path"....

Non-natives were often astonished when an Indian scout declared that a mountain lion was on the prowl in the vicinity. If the Indian were asked, "Have you seen it?" he would respond, "No, it's written on the ground!"

When it came to the art of communication, the Indian had many resources to draw on. General Connor learned this the hard way when he took the Bozeman Trail through Dakota territory in the 1860s. Charged with a punitive mission against the Oglala Dakota, the party had been traveling since morning. In front, a Hunkpapa scout led the way, indulging in remarkable displays of horsemanship. He halted his mount, flew off at a gallop, and whirled around just as a large band of Indians charged from behind the hills and spread death among the Bluecoats.

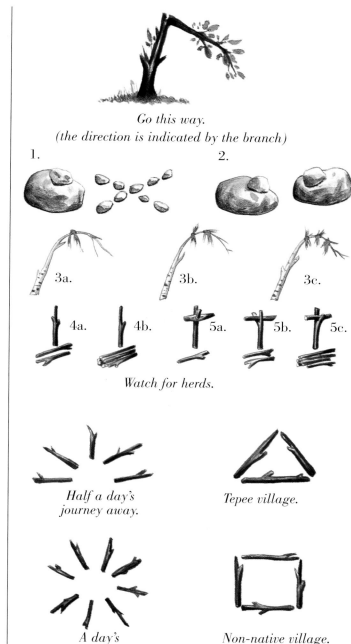

Go this way.
(the direction is indicated by the branch)

Watch for herds.

Half a day's journey away.

Tepee village.

A day's journey away.

Non-native village.

1. Behind a hill, a large herd. 2. Stampeding herd. 3a. One bison seen. 3b. Two bisons seen. 3c. Herd seen (In the direction indicated by the branch). 4a. Two enemy Indians spotted. 4b. Enemy tribe spotted. 5a. One white man seen. 5b. Two white men seen. 5c. A white regiment seen.

Diagrammatic representation of a tepee. This figure is found on numerous ornaments.

When the Body Tells a Story

Many Indians traced a wide variety of designs onto their bodies. Some of these designs were messages, prayers to the gods, or exorcisms of evil spirits. These "body paintings" narrated things about a person, her tribe, and the circumstances of her life. Many Indians felt fearful and uneasy faced with the impressive displays of thunderstorms, believing that they personified powerful spirits. An Indian might paint lightning on his chest to invoke and take on its power. A hand painted on her shoulder suggested that the Great Spirit had placed a paternal hand there in a protective gesture. The print of a bear's paw on his thigh confirmed that he truly was Ma-to-tchee-ga, Growling Bear, and that he possessed the ill-tempered character of the animal. To be alone with their thoughts, some Indians drew a black line across their foreheads so that no one would disturb them.

On his return to the fort, Connor related his astonishment to the veteran scout Jim Bridger. Old Jim, married to an Indian woman, gave him the explanation: "Probably the ones who ambushed you were watching your scout, who communicated to his friends the number of your soldiers, their weapons, your destination and your purpose by changing the speed of his pony, making it perform in the way you saw. Thanks to your scouts, the Indians knew that they could attack you without incurring too many casualties."

As the Indian scouts had vanished in the confrontation, General Connor swore to stop using Indian scouts and recruited the services of old Bridger himself.

The first non-native settlers certainly believed that Indians had red skin (hence the epithet "Redskin"), perhaps because Indians often painted or tattooed their skin, or because the skin of the color-conscious Europeans had very little pigment. It is obvious that many Indians have slightly brown skin, with the exception of some Northeastern tribes like the Iroquois, whose skin color resembles that of northern Europeans. Of course, Indians' skin has never been any more red than that of anyone else. Some indigenous people coated their skin liberally with the juice of an inedible fruit, called "roucou" in South America, which produces a deep red juice. Living half-naked outdoors, Indians protected themselves against the attacks of all kinds of insects (fleas, ticks, mosquitoes, etc.)

with the help of repeated applications of many ointments, including the vermilion colored roucou, mixed with animal fat. This substance blocked the pores and prevented certain parasites from attaching themselves to the skin, thus preventing Indians from catching insect-borne illnesses.

Ideograms

Many Indians used ideograms to decorate their clothes, shields, arrows, tepees, and other objects of daily life.

The paintings on the shafts of arrows indicated who had shot them. Did they bear three red circles? If so they came from the Onondaga tribe, the third Iroquois nation, under the protection of fire! The Wah-kee, the Dakota shield, bore multi-colored paintings that generally narrated dreams or significant events in the owner's life. The outside of a tepee gave information about its occupant. An elk painted on the skin might indicate courage and quiet strength: a sparrowhawk, clear sight and endurance.

The Comanches loved to cover the hides of wild sheep and deer with colorful designs that might contain details of a battle, like the spot where it took place and the number of victims.

In 1821, the Cherokee Se-quoy-ah created an alphabet, or, more properly, a syllabary, adapted to his own language. The Cherokee soon began publishing a journal using these symbols. Later, in 1930, the Navaho brought out a monthly revue. But as their audience was mostly illiterate, this initiative quickly died.

The river of life

From birth to death all Indians went
through a succession of stages marked
by initiation ceremonies. Native Americans
did not view death as an ending.
They spent their lives preparing
for it, happy to travel to an
eternal paradise.

As long ago the Great Spirit had traced river
courses across the land and through the valleys,
so it guided the destiny of the small child.

The Win (Women)

Even when the men sprawled about, their backs firmly propped against their "backrests," serenely smoking their pipes, camp nonetheless seemed to bustle with activity. If they were good hunters some Indian men could marry as many women as they could feed. Women took on most domestic tasks, while men saved themselves mainly for diplomacy, hunting, and war. To him, all other tasks seemed beneath his dignity and not his responsibility.

The win fetched water from the river, collected wood, lit the fire, dried the meat, prepared the meals, sewed, embroidered, tanned and chewed the skins to soften them, looked after the children, gathered wild plant foods, put up and took down the dwellings, gathered the dogs and horses to harness them, and, if she had any strength left over, she packed the baggage when the tribe moved to follow the bison herds or to change locations. The men, for their part, led the way and provided an escort! But we should not be misled by this. When men went hunting, they took part in exhausting chases, and ran the constant risk of revenge attacks from large vindictive animals. Supplying the family with meat brought its own risks, and war was no less dangerous.

Made from two planks with curved ends, the "toboggan" – also called the "wilderness sled" by the people of the north – glided easily over the frozen rivers and the snow-covered ground.

The Papoose

Some Indian women carried their babies on their back in a narrow cradle. The child, comfortably installed and held in place by hide thongs, stayed there until she could walk. In winter, on their snowshoes, which they could not take off lest their feet sink in the powdery snow, northern Indians went on long journeys without suffering from the aching hips that afflicted most of the non-natives.

The traditional extended family structure meant that a child was often raised by one of her aunts, if it was a girl, or by an uncle if it was a boy. The child spent most of her time adding to her store of knowledge. The Wise Old Ones taught her the tribe's religion, ways, and customs. By watching them she learned the fundamentals of her future occupations.

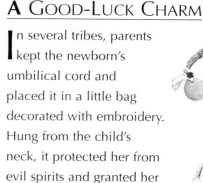

A GOOD-LUCK CHARM

In several tribes, parents kept the newborn's umbilical cord and placed it in a little bag decorated with embroidery. Hung from the child's neck, it protected her from evil spirits and granted her a peaceful life.

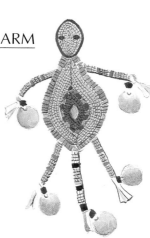

The win found a practical way to entertain her infant. With a simple movement of her knee, the amulet swung from side to side and kept the child amused.

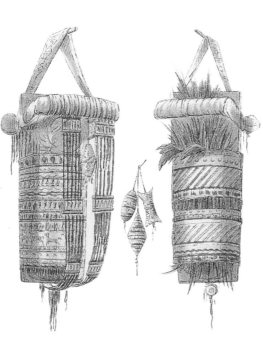

Infant mortality was relatively high among Native Americans. When a child died, some mothers continued to carry its cradle on her back for a whole snow. As a sign of mourning, she filled the basket with black bird feathers, or alternatively, with soft grass.

THE USEFULNESS OF TOYS

Everything presented an opportunity to learn. Thus, a doll was not only a toy for a little girl. She dressed it and embroidered its clothes, as she would later have to do for herself.

THE STORYTELLER

In the past, among the Indians of North America, traditions were passed on orally in the evenings around the camp fire. In the form of legends retold by their elders, the young people learned the rules of life and the foundations of their tribe's own philosophy. Legends of a supernatural nature were told after sunset. No stranger or non-native was permitted to hear them. Only those stories concerned with ordinary daily life could be heard by everyone.

Among the Indians of the Great Lakes, young girls gathered reeds and grasses while the women wove mats and bags. Among the Plains Indians, boys guarded the horses while hunters, hidden in the high ground, watched the movement of bison herds. In the evenings, seated by the fire, adolescents would listen to the Guardians Of The Great Things Of The Past re-telling the legends of the Ancestors In the Darkness.

A child had the right to make mistakes and was never punished for tantrums or other lapses in behavior.

Among some tribes, custom dictated that once a year young children could indulge in the most outrageous pranks: stamping out a fire, putting water in a man's pipe, putting itching powder down her mother's back....

Unfortunately this amnesty only lasted as long as one sun!

THE TRAIL OF THE YOUNG WARRIORS

At the age of about thirteen, boys of the Great Plains were called to the hard life of a nomadic warrior. Some took part in an initiation destined to measure their physical stamina, their endurance of pain, and their complete understanding of nature. The war chiefs informed the young man of the place he had to go, sometimes over 50 miles away, the route he should follow at all costs, the objects he would find on the way and with which he had to return, as well as the time allowed to him to cover the Trail of the Young Warriors, in both directions.

Those Who Know recounted to the young boy all the difficulties he would encounter along the way: the baking hot desert, the snow-covered peaks, the impassable rapids, the dried-up river beds, and the venomous snakes. They also advised him to conserve his strength and to look after his mount if he wished to return proudly on horseback in a brightly colored robe.

Before his departure the adolescent took a gourd of water to slake his horse's thirst, and one mouthful for himself, which he had to keep in his mouth throughout the whole test, and spit out before his judges on his return.

The adolescent who passed his initiation was given the title, Young Man Of Inexhaustible Resources. He was then able to enter a special society where the Initiation of the Warriors awaited him.

The Initiation of the Warriors

A post about 15 feet high was planted in the ground. Plaited leather straps hung from its top. To the side, the future initiates had been fasting for four days in a specially furnished hut. They were enclosed there in secrecy with the shaman, and no one was able to see them.

At the beginning of the fourth day, the whole tribe assembled around the tall pole. The skull of a bison killed in the recent hunts swung from it. The entrance of the hut opened and the sorcerer emerged, followed by the future warriors. Once the candidates for initiation were in their places, the shaman turned toward them. He took out his knife and his assistant showed off two hardwood pegs. The first volunteer came forward while the regular sound of Mystery-Whistles rose in the clear morning.

The shaman pinched the skin of his left pectoral between two fingers, pulled and passed his knife through the flesh, from one side to the other. The assistant inserted a peg, which stuck out an inch or two on either side. The process was repeated for the right pectoral. The young men could ask for more pegs to be put into their backs, calves, thighs, and biceps. The more they demanded, the more they showed their courage and the more proud they could be. The sorcerer then attached straps to the pegs. The fearless young man had to lean back to draw the cords tight and bend the pole like a spring.

At no time was he able to complain. At the first groan, the first sign of weakness, he was detached from the pole and became an ordinary person again. He would try again next year....

AUTHENTICITY

The painter George Catlin witnessed one of these ceremonies and made several sketches of it from life. Fearing that he would be accused of falsehood, he asked the two people who accompanied him to give him a certificate of verification. This is the text of that certificate: "We the undersigned certify that we were present, in company with Mr Catlin, in the Mandan village, at the ceremonies depicted in four of his drawings and paintings and described in his notes. We confirm, by this certificate, that he has faithfully represented the scenes, as we saw them unfold, without addition or exaggeration."

J. Kipp, Agent of the American Fur Company.

L. Crawford, employee. Abraham Bogart. Mandan village, 20 July 1833.

After about an hour, the initiate's agony was cut short by the shaman's assistants who laid the new warrior on the ground so that he could regain his strength. No one could help him get up, or else he would have truly died. The injured man's friends and family were not allowed to dress his wounds: a good soul would bring him healing herbs and soothing ointment later. By offering this sacrifice to the Great Spirit, the Indian placed himself under its protection.

The candidate for initiation left his family and friends. In silence and tranquility, he took stock of the strength he would need to endure his future trials.

The Last Race

After this first initiation, the strongest were allowed to progress to the ultimate test: the Last Race.

The Warriors of the Last Race were led to the village square. There, two strapping men flanked each candidate, took him by the wrists and, to the sound of drums, began running in large circles. The young man, already weakened, let himself be pulled along. Then, having run out of strength, he collapsed. But the men grabbed him again, attached lines to the pegs and set off once more, pulling with all their strength. The youth was dragged along the ground, his wounds getting bigger until at last the skin tore open.

Only at this point was he allowed to return unaided to his tepee. The shaman praised him, stating that at no point had he uttered the slightest cry. The one who withstood the ordeal best, the most valiant, took a name that was the envy of all. He became, Nah-se-us-kuk, Rolling Thunder! Music and shouts of encouragement from the excited crowd helped him to bear the pain. The evening saw his consecration as he was accorded the status of Exceptional Man!

THE TRIAL OF THE SUN

Among the Ting-ta-to-ah, another tribe in the Siovan family, when a brave warrior decided that his medicine was stronger than the others', he asked the sorcerer to "fix the sun." The shaman proceeded to slit just one pectoral, and the young man, with his body constantly leaning backward, pulled on the line.

In this uncomfortable position, he had to keep his face turned toward the sun. He moved around the pole in order to follow the sun's path.

And if, at its setting, the man had not turned away for an instant, the elders came to cut him down and heal him with medical herbs. Throughout the day, he would have been encouraged by his friends who continually exhorted him and placed offerings to his success at the foot of the pole.

Union

A SOUTHWESTERN MARRIAGE RITE

Among the Navaho, a man who married a woman who had been rejected by a previous husband sometimes offered her a dress as a sign of magnanimity. When the wife died, her best friends dressed her body in the garment.

Marriage customs varied from tribe to tribe. Among some groups, when a man reached the age of marriage, often between fifteen and twenty years old, and, most importantly, when he was rich enough to take a wife, the suitor sought out the parents of the girl he desired. Together they smoked pipes filled with the future husband's tobacco and conducted a detailed negotiation. The agreement concluded, a friend of the suitor, who was in on the secret, arrived with presents. If the parents decided the gifts were insufficient, the friend went off to find more. If they were accepted, the man led the woman into his tepee.

If he was not completely satisfied with the woman, he could always return her to her family. But then endless discussions ensued, in which the husband could never be certain of regaining possession of his gifts. When the young wife had good teeth for chewing the hides and she did not shirk at the domestic work, her husband would promise her that in case of adultery he would not slit her nose or throw her out of the tribe. Among the Matrilineal Iroquois, women were particularly influential. They selected the chiefs, sat at the councils, and could decide whether or not the tribe went to war. Women were in charge of most village activities, including marriage. Their power was based in part on the fact that they provided the essentials of life: the "three sisters" of corn, beans and squash.

Toward the Eternal Land of the Dead

Particularly before they acquired horses, some Plains Indians abandoned their elderly people. Grown old and feeling his end approaching, the man who had not been lucky enough to die out hunting or in battle and who found it too shameful to die of an illness in his bed, called his family and close friends together and told them, "The migration of the bison is coming. You must leave for new hunting grounds, and follow the herds to avoid dying of starvation. I am old and worn out and you are young. If I wanted to follow you on the trail, I would only slow you down. My eyes can hardly see and my legs can no longer carry me. I wish to be 'exposed' as I myself exposed my father and my mother long ago. I have spoken. How!"

Then his children might erect an old tent and place the aged one inside it. They lit a small fire and took care to leave him a little tobacco and a few provisions. Then the tribe moved away for a new hunt. This was the Exposing of the Old Ones, a rite that answered the wish of everyone to be able to choose the day of his death. The ancestor, thus left alone in the abandoned village in the middle of the vast prairie, was exposed to the eyes of the Great Spirit, to whom he gave up his soul. After the visits of wolves, coyotes, foxes, and birds of prey, when the tribe returned that way the following year, the children looked for the bones of their abandoned parents. They collected them and placed them reverently in a skin bag pending the building of a funerary scaffold or a visit to the sacred mountains where they could bury them under a mound.

Among the sedentary Mandans the funeral rites were different: the old people died surrounded by their nearest and dearest. When a death approached, the shaman was called. At the person's bedside, he uttered an initial prayer, begging the corpse to come back to life. When the deceased did not respond, he began a wild dance jumping and whirling to the sound of bells and rattles. These contortions could last several hours, at the end of which he commanded the corpse to get up. When it once again refused to move, the shaman ordered everyone to leave so that he could consult in private with Wa-kan-da (a name for the Great Spirit). No one was allowed to be present at the interview. In front of the entrance, the relatives and friends waited. After these

SAYING FAREWELL TO SOULS

If the dying person had not yet given up her soul, the shaman of some tribes entered her hut with his small-medicine. This generally consisted of bells and rattles made from dry fruit. He commanded the assembly to intone chants that help to restore life, and he himself uttered a few incantations to the rhythm of his instruments. If it became clear that the patient was in the throes of death and if by ill luck she expired, the sorcerer brought out his big medicine. He put on a bear costume that covered him from head to foot. All sorts of talismans hung from his shoulders and his neck, such as lynx claws, pike fins, snake fangs, dried owls' eyes, elk hooves, owl beaks and eagle talons.

In 1904, after living through the ravages of war and the theft of his people's land, Thunder Which Rolls in the Mountains, Chief Joseph, dies surrounded by his family on a Washington reserve.

MOURNING

Many Native Americans communicated their feelings in a heartfelt yet ritualistic way. On the death of a child or a beloved spouse, a man or a woman externalized her suffering. Some went as far as self-mutilation. To convey his unhappiness, he might remain prostrate for a whole day, his limbs pierced through, showing off his pain. The deeper and more unbearable his sorrow, the greater the display of pain.

A young woman mourns for her husband, exposed at the top of an escarpment. The body of the warrior and that of his favorite horse, sacrificed for the occasion, will rest there for eternity.

incantations the sorcerer came out and announced that the deceased wished to stay in the Land of the Dead, that the Great Spirit agreed with this wish and that no one could dispute it. Having announced with this death to which the Great Spirit freely gave its consent and acceptance, the shaman's responsibilities were fulfilled.

Then the chorus of lamentation began. Friends scratched their faces until they bled, the whole tribe wept and asked Wa-kan-da to open the doors of paradise to the valorous deceased, and to send a new soul from heaven to replace that of the departed. The deceased was then wrapped in a bison skin with his most treasured possessions. With four branches from which the bark had been stripped away, her friends raised a funerary scaffold in the Mandan cemetery. They fixed a platform on the poles and placed the corpse there so that it would not become the prey of scavengers. In a final act of homage, a dead man's favorite dogs and horses were killed and their heads placed on the pillars of the funerary scaffold.

In this way, after his death the Indian returned the best things that Wa-kan-da had bestowed on him during his passage on earth.

The Assiniboins did not bury their dead.
These Forest Indians placed the deceased and the
objects to which he had been attached in the
branches of a tree.
This Exposure of the Dead, adopted for reasons
of hygiene, protected the remains from predators.

The voice of wisdom

For many Indian groups, the word "chief" had only a distant relationship to the meaning given it by the non-native. With significant exceptions, Native Americans were endowed with an unshakable sense of

personal

independence,

although their

actions were often

constrained by custom.

Most chiefs did not give orders.

They were chosen according to their

human attributes, their experience, their

wisdom, and their patience. Some chiefs

also inherited their offices. Either way,

important decisions were usually made by the

tribal councils.

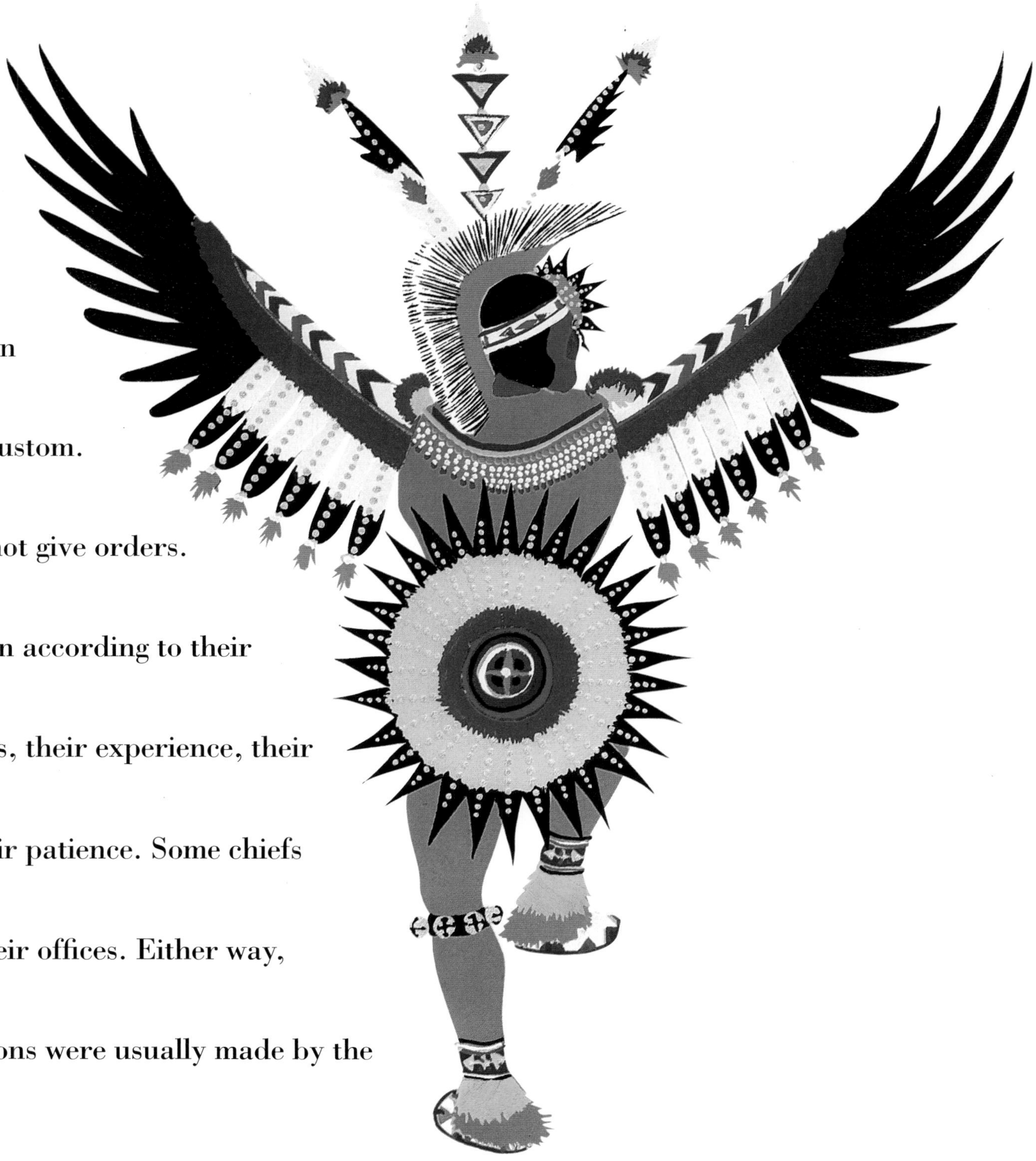

Social and Political Organization

These Mandan elders, Si-oh-oh, Single View, and Wat-iou-eh, Man of Dreams, steered their people away from starting a futile war that would have lasted more than four hundred years.

Non-natives have given Indians many bad labels over the years: savage, barbarian, ugly, ignorant… through his habits and his apparent nonchalance, the Indian could in fact seem uncultured and disorganized. But one should remember that the Iroquois League was so well structured that in 1776 the first government of the United States based its constitution in part on that of the "savages." The following are examples of the political and social systems of some Native American people. The Natchez who belonged to the inferior caste were called the Stinkard. In modern times we still find a similar social structure in India.

In the South, the Natchez were divided into two classes: the aristocracy and the people. All were governed by a potentate called Sun. The Natchez held him in high esteem and proclaimed his power. His servants followed him in the grave, in the same way as the ancient Egyptians.

The Dené lived in Canada. This large family was the origin of numerous tribes, the best known of which are the Navaho and the Apache. The Zuni were divided into clans that were completely separate from each other. Marriage to someone in the same clan or one's father was prohibited. Like many native people, Zunis observed the mother-in-law taboo: the son-in-law could not look at or speak directly to his mother-in-law.

At the center of a vast land, many groups adopted parallel war and peace political structures. Some Plains Indians, for example, could not conceive that the same leader could take decisions on diametrically opposed issues. For them, war and peace required the knowledge of two different specialists. As the spiritual side of life was paramount for Native Americans, participation in the council of a holy person was often essential. The divergent opinions of these different leaders explained the slow pace of negotiations in a council at least as perceived by non-natives. Furthermore, councils were not run by majority rule—decisions had to be unanimous. Interminable discussions went on, and the whites became impatient.

THE WAR CHIEF

The war chief owed his position to his valor and his victories. His fame raised him to this position that was the envy of the younger men. His role consisted of raising aspirations and in setting a good example for future warriors in search of daring feats to accomplish. The war chief evaluated the advantages of a military engagement for his tribe. If such an engagement was a long time coming, he presented himself to the council of elders with strong arguments: "My brothers, our warriors have been living like women for as many moons as there are leaves in the trees. Feared and renowned for our bravery, we are covered in shame. My heart bleeds, my eyes fill with tears when I think that our enemies are laughing at our weakness. Soon they will denounce us for our indolence. You, the elders, who know how brave were our fathers and their fathers' fathers, will you tolerate this insult much longer? Our young men speak of letting themselves die of hunger. Shall we let our fiercest warriors die a shameful death? I await your response. I have spoken."

Who, even among the most stubborn, would not have pondered on these words? Having persuaded the elders, the war chief was obliged to behave valiantly, or else a young challenger might take away his title.

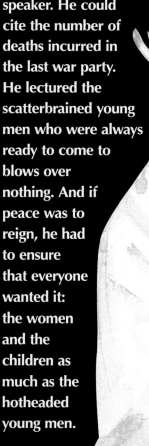

It should be noted that the war chief never gave orders, as the Indians would not have welcomed them. To give an order was regarded as dishonorable as giving in to the will of another. At the start of a confrontation, it would have been enough for Geronimo to shout, "Forward, into battle!" for the warriors to put their hands over their mouths and think, "Who does this man think he is, to dare to give an order to another man?" Taken aback, they would no doubt have stayed in their places and Geronimo would have ridden into the attack alone. Indian leaders led by example and they were followed because – and while – they embodied the values of their people.

Discipline was maintained by example, and that is one reason most Indians had only a moderate respect for the President of the United States. They called him, among other names, He Who Does Not Go To War With His Men.

THE PEACE CHIEF

The peace chief was in normal circumstances an old man, rich in experience and moderation. The people of the tribe did not elect him, but they supported him if he was generous, just, accomplished, personable, and a good speaker. He could cite the number of deaths incurred in the last war party. He lectured the scatterbrained young men who were always ready to come to blows over nothing. And if peace was to reign, he had to ensure that everyone wanted it: the women and the children as much as the hotheaded young men.

GERONIMO

The Apache Geronimo, from his real name, Go-ya-leh (Open Mouth), was raised among whites by a Methodist pastor called Sam Flaherty. One Sunday he stole a horse and ran away to rejoin his tribe. Later, he became war chief and head of the Chiricahua tribe. Geronimo eventually became the scourge of the U.S. army. He and his men monopolized the attention of 5,000 Yankee soldiers for six years. They halted the colonization of the Southwest for years. His raids terrorized the wagon trains and traders: the Santa Fe trail was cut, three stagecoach companies went bust, the Pony Express was re-routed, eastern pioneers refused to go to California, and trade suffered. When he gave himself up because of lack of ammunition, the leader of the Chiricahuas agreed to go to live in the San Carlos reserve in Arizona. Later, he was sent to a Florida prisoner-of-war camp. Before his death in 1909, Geronimo became a successful farmer and dictated his autobiography.

Geronimo (on horseback), with his son and grandson. On returning from a hunt the Chiricahua chief found his whole family had been killed: the whites had committed another mass murder.

Would they cooperate or resist? The war chief argued for the pressing need for a battle. The peace chief knew that good decisions were never made in haste. Other leaders examined the social implications and the Shaman consulted the spirits to discover where the truth lay. After two or three days of thoughtful discussion the decision was given to the frantic whites.

When he wanted to relay a prophetic message, Coo-coo-coo, The Owl, smoked the feathered pipe. This sacred pipe invoked the eagle, the messenger of the Great Spirit. Its exceptionally long stem could be dismantled into several sections. The old Iroquois elder said that visions came to him while the smoke was rising to his mouth.

THE LANGUAGE OF FEATHERS

Many Native Americans valued feathers, partly because of their association with spiritual powers. Reserved exclusively for men, feather ornaments added to their imposing bearing and elegance. A jay's wing, for instance, might designate a high-ranking individual.

The Tribal Chief

In most cases, the word "tribe" is a non-native invention. In the spirit of egalitarianism and/or because it was easier to acquire food, many Indians were organized into bands, or local groups, or autonomous villages, each of which had a chief. Few true "tribes" emerged until the immediate pre-reservation period, if then. Nevertheless, non-natives persist in thinking in terms of a tribe with a tribal chief, who was not looked on as a monarch. The council of elders selected him for a very specific job. Most important was that his people admired his

When a leader agreed to sell tribal lands or declared that his people would live in peace, he was given a gift such as a ribbon on which hung a medal cast with the image of the "Grandfather President." The bigger the medal, the greater had been the Indian's sacrifice. The leader became recognized by the non-natives as a "good Indian."

The Wampum (from the Iroquois wam: message and pum: written) was used to seal verbal agreements. As a sign of allegiance, the Wyandot, or Hurons, gave the Frenchman Frontenac a wampum belt of black and white beads (a sign of peace), representing the tribe's four great divisions.

LEGENDARY FIGURES

In their historic struggles for survival, many Indians, some well known and some anonymous, rose to the status of head. The oglala Red Cloud led the temporarily successful campaign to close the Boleman trail. With his victory, he forced the U.S. to sign the Fort Laramie treaty of 1868.

Cochise was an important Chiricahua Apache war chief. He surrendered in 1872 only after winning assurances that he and his band could remain in the Chiricahua mountains. Black Kettle, the Southern Cheyennes' peace chief, consistently held out for peace, even after the infamous Sand Creek massacre of 1869. Thunder Which Rolls in the Mountains, the famous Chief Joseph, helped lead his peaceful people on an epic 1,500 mile-flight to Canada. He was forced to surrender just 30 miles from the border, on which occasion he gave a famous speech. He later encouraged his people to attend schools run by non-natives.

Cochise on his horse with his son Natchez.

integrity, his experience and his impartiality. He played the role of arbitrator when a difference arose among members of the tribe.

He had to ensure that his people were always provided with food. He therefore had to have a perfect knowledge of nature and of the seasons in which the herds moved or the crops grew. On the Plains, if the lookouts spotted Ta-tan-ka, the bison, the chief played a large role in directing the hunt. He decided the number of beasts to be killed, and on the return of the hunters, he divided the skins and the meat, taking into consideration the widows, orphans, old people, and invalids who were the responsibility of the tribe. It was also he who gave the signal for departure on the long marches that the people made each year when the herds migrated.

THE HEADDRESS OF THE CHIEFS

The Dakota kept the eagle-feather bonnet mainly for ceremonies. A small headdress hung down the back as far as the shoulder blades and a large one occasionally touched the heels. Warriors often decorated it with the scalps of their enemies.

The tribal chief signed the treaties with the Blue Tunics of the Yankee army. (Of course, when there was no tribal chief, band or local chiefs signed. This custom allowed non-natives to suppose that a band leader could represent an entire people and, thus, that a treaty signed with just one group was binding on the whole Indian nation. The Indians, for their part, never understood why non-natives acted as though one band leader represented many independent groups.) This elder was the representative, the word, and the seal of his people. He had to be both responsible and diplomatic. And if his fame was not as spectacularly won as that of some others, his opinion prevailed over all. In the council, his vote could tip the balance even if everyone expressed a different opinion. Like the other chiefs, he did not give orders, which was beyond the comprehension of non-natives.

The Power of Women

Roles and responsibilities differed from one nation to another. If the Dakota men seemed to have scant consideration for their wives, Iroquois revered theirs. Women were able to judge some situations more objectively. When the question arose of going to make war against the Hurons, the Iroquois women were fully aware of the consequences that the clashes would bring: some men would return lying inside the canoes.

Several women endowed with great knowledge and integrity, and with agile minds, achieved great fame, holding the titles of tribal chief and war chief at the same time. Among the Iroquois, women were always the clan leaders and, as such, wielded considerable power.

In the Wichita tribe, male and female virgins held important positions in the councils. When they occupied these roles, they were called, respectively, Wi-as-uks, He Who Has Loved No Woman, and Mi-ti-li, She Who Has Loved No Man.

Worn by the Plains Indians and long mistakenly regarded as a piece of protective armor, the deer-bone breastplate's sole function was to indicate the prestige of its wearer.

THE STAFF OF MERCY

The warrior, armed with his staff, goes into a battle where for once blood is not shed. In this parody of war, he gains respect and honor, in the same way as if he had killed many enemies.

From one snow to another

Indian habits and customs were influenced by the place and the climatic conditions that prevailed in the area where they lived. Nature provided the foundation from which many Native Americans developed rich and complex cultures.

The Village

Indian villages were often located near water. Some were built in strategic locations, such as hilltops or protected valleys. Villages might be small, with only a few houses or they might be filled with hundreds or even thousands of people.

The Plains tribes, who were essentially nomadic, set up their villages near the migration routes of the bison herds. The collection of tepees always formed a circle, the most holy of sacred forms. It was the symbol of the interconnectedness of the universe.

The Apache Wickiup

In former times, the Apaches were the warrior-protectors—as well as the antagonists—of the Pueblo people. They formed several great tribes, including the Chiricahuas, the Jicarius, and Mescalerus. They learned to tame herds of wild horses. As nomads, they adopted a wandering lifestyle.

The Apache always had to be ready to flee. For this reason, her house, the wickiup, was made from a frame of branches. This shelter made an ideal camouflage in case of attack. The Apache regarded her wickiup as a simple refuge, destined to be destroyed or easily replaced.

Multi-Story Houses

From west to east and from north to south, each Indian group has its own ideas about living conditions. In the south, near the border with Mexico, the Hopi and Pueblo Indians constructed multi-story houses made of wooden frames and a mixture of clay and straw (adobe). The inhabitants of these dwellings climbed to the higher floors using large wooden ladders. In the evening, these were drawn up for safety. These sedentary Indians, more farmers than hunters, used conical clay ovens to cook the loaves made from maize flour, their staple diet. Each home possessed a kiva. This is a medicine room, a sort of chapel where dancers place the sacred dolls, the Kat-chi-na, used at religious ceremonies.

Pueblo Indian houses were terraced. The only means of access were ladders, easy to draw up in case of attack.

Before the arrival of non-natives, the Hopis and Navahos wove coarse cloth on looms of their own design. Today they use similar tools to make colorful blankets and traditional ponchos, which non-native traders sell at a high price in the towns. Lightweight cotton fabric, introduced by the non-natives, was welcome in this sun-parched part of the world.

The Wigwam

At the time of the battles between the French and the English for possession of North America, there lived in the Northeast several powerful Indian nations, the most famous of which were the Hurons, the Iroquois, and the Chippewas (Anishinabe). These Indians, who were fishermen, hunters, and gardeners, had adopted a semi-sedentary lifestyle. They erected palisades around their kitchen gardens where they planted tomatoes, beans, pumpkins, maize (corn), potatoes, and tobacco. These Forest Indians built their villages on the

The Wyandot, or Hurons, built villages that resembled those of the Iroquois. They, also, raised walls of wood to protect their various crops.

THE "THREE SISTERS"

The Iroquois cultivated the Three Sisters, that is, beans, squash, and maize (corn). They planted the maize at regular distances apart so that the stems could serve as supports for the beans. Squash grew between the maize plants. Maize was consumed in various ways: grilled, it was enjoyed with maple syrup and animal fat.

banks of rivers and lakes and at the edges of the great forests of red cedar, maple, and birch. They used these trees in the construction of their wigwams. Supple arched branches arranged like upturned baskets on the ground were both watertight and very stable. The frameworks, covered with birch bark, were topped with a smoke hole. A second opening served as an entrance. The people used these very comfortable wigwams for eating meals, sleeping, and receiving friends.

The Long Houses

The Kanonsionni, or League of the United Households, better known under the name Iroquois, often built dwellings that were over 100 feet long by 15 feet wide. A characteristic of the nation, they could house ten families, sometimes more. Low platforms, running along the inner walls, were used as beds. The longhouse was also a symbol of the League of the Five Nations, formed in the 15th or 16th century through the joining of five allied tribes. According to the metaphor, the Mohawk were the "Keepers of the Eastern Door" of the longhouse, while the Seneca guarded the western door. The Tuscaroras joined the five original nations in the early 18th century. Villages were often protected by palisades of pointed stakes. Lookouts guarded the crops day and night.

The Mandan Hut

Further west, between the Mississippi River and the Rocky Mountains, on a vast prairie more than 2,000 miles in length from north to south, lived the Plains Indians. Although most of these Indians were nomads, the Mandans lived a sedentary lifestyle. To construct his house, the Mandan dug into the earth to a depth of around two to three feet, forming a circle about 40 feet in diameter. A six-foot-high frame of logs was covered with layers of branches, sod, and earth. The roof possessed a smoke hole that also allowed light to enter. The walls of these lodges were very thick, and supported a roof so strong that it could be used as a terrace for large gatherings! This dwelling provided equal protection from the cold and from the heat.

Talismans, fixed on the ends of long poles, kept the evil spirits away and allowed the Mandans to carry on their agricultural and trade activities.

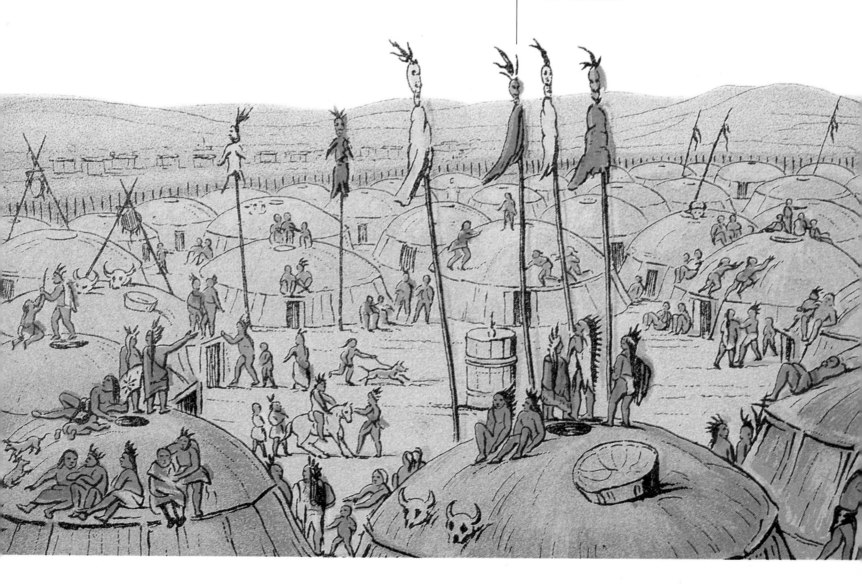

The Blackfeet erected tepees made from buckskin or caribou hide. These tents, properly aligned, presented a completely vertical face to the prevailing wind, whereas the construction as a whole was gently sloping. Sheltered from gusts of wind, these tepees could withstand the most violent snowstorms.

Tepees

To the West of Mandan territory lay the hunting grounds of the Crow. These people lived in tepees. The tepee, a large conical tent, was constructed from a framework of poles placed in a circle that joined at the top. This structure supported a covering of bison or elk skins sewn together. Wooden pegs closed the final seam. To take it down all the people had to do was pull out the pegs and let the covering slide onto the poles. The uprights served as frames for the travois or wheel-less carts harnessed to dogs and, later, to horses. At the bottom of the tepee a gap provided an entrance. At the top, there was a triangular vent between large, adjustable "ventilation flaps." This funneled the smoke from the central fireplace and prevented it from blowing back over the occupants. Crow tepees were often painted with pictures of the owner's war feats.

The Inside of the Tepee

Non-natives may enter their houses without taking precautions, scorning all conventions, but the Dakota has more respect for her living space. The tepee is round, and all round things are sacred to these people. When a visitor wishes to enter a tepee, she scratches three times on the skin of the tent, and on the invitation of her host, crosses the threshold. She always walks around the circle to the left. When the owner of the dwelling is standing at the right of the entrance, the visitor traces a complete circle, in the direction of the sun's path, to walk up to her. To cover the short distance in a straight line would cause grave offense to the host and attract the curses of evil spirits to the dwelling.

Forest Indian Satchel

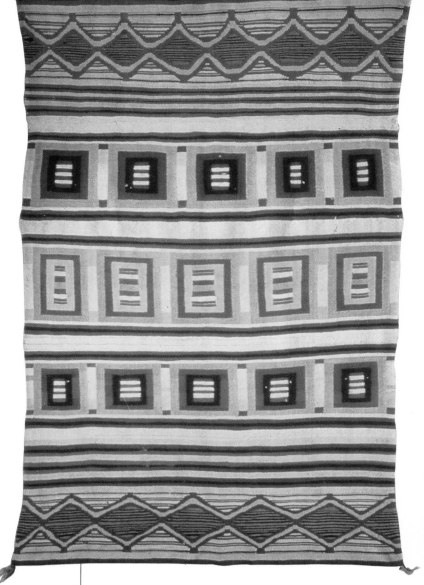

Navaho carpet from New Mexico

Ornamental item originating in the Great Lakes area, in painted openwork leather and adorned with horsehair tassels.

The interior of the Mandan house is comparable to a tepee. There is plenty of storage space for various tools.

SNOWSHOES

Still used in Canada and in the northern United States, snowshoes are made of a hoop, usually of ash wood, bent so that it forms an oval. The frame is threaded with a network of cord or gut,

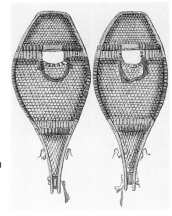

which is interlaced and imperishable. The central fastening should only hold the end of the foot, so that the heel is able to lift up normally at the end of each step. When used, snowshoes caused a pain in the hips, "snowshoe ache,"

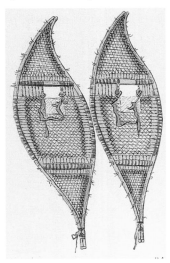

because they forced the wearer to walk with his legs apart. While other Indians liked short, stubby snowshoes, called "bears' paws," the Iroquois preferred a long shape, and Micmacs used a square-ended version.

At the center of the tepee, stones arranged in a circle protected the fireplace. Above this, a tripod supported a cooking pot or a can. This receptacle always contained food. The sign of welcome being, "Are you hungry?" it was important at all times to be able to provide for any chance visitor. Soft furs were arranged on the ground. The whole family, including near relations and close friends, could sleep in an average-size tepee. They lay with their heads close to the walls of the tent and their feet toward the fire, like the rays of the sun.

The inside of the tepee was cozy and comfortable, and it was richly decorated with objects arranged on the ground or hung from poles. Wooden pegs sunk into the uprights allowed the people to hang shields, quivers, bags, clubs, and badges of honor. Many of these objects were adorned with feathers and decorated with multi-colored porcupine quills, and were the wonder of all who saw them.

On the ground, rawhide chests, called "arrow guards," were used to store ceremonial robes. Eagle feather bonnets were kept in special boxes called Headdress Cases. Other trunks contained the ornaments and religious objects needed for ritual dances. All these items bore paintings designed to keep away evil influences. Ritual as well as everyday pipes were stored in bags made from otter, marten, mink, or ermine skins. These precious objects were often embroidered and beaded.

The Backrest

Many plains groups used a unique piece of furniture to increase their level of comfort. The backrest was made from round pieces of wood linked by a leather thong. It measured about four feet long and two feet wide. Placed on the ground, the upper three-quarters of the backrest was supported by three wooden poles about three feet long. Indians could simply sit on the horizontal section and rest their backs against the vertical part. Rolled up, this seat took up a small amount of space and could be transported easily.

Sitting comfortably, a man would smoke pipe after pipe. With his back well-supported, he could attend the council, even if it lasted two days. To one side, on another backrest, his wife threaded bartered beads on bone needles and decorated ceremonial costumes.

KEEPING WARM IN THE TEPEE

The tepee offered numerous advantages. Moved to a new site in the summer, it allowed the ground to make a complete recovery. In winter, the Season When The Wolves Hunt in Packs, the temperature drops by up to 100 or more degrees. To improve the tepee's insulation, people prepared a "curtain wall," or inner layer of skin. Women fed the central fire day and night with wood or dried bison dung. Men often had little work to do in winter.

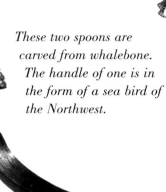

These two spoons are carved from whalebone. The handle of one is in the form of a sea bird of the Northwest.

Food

Most Indians spent the bulk of their time engaged in food-related activities. Whether farmer or hunter, sedentary or nomadic, obtaining provisions was more important than anything. Even war itself had to be fought on a full stomach. Among some tribes, when someone invited you to eat, he did not eat with you. Women served the

Woven rush basket.

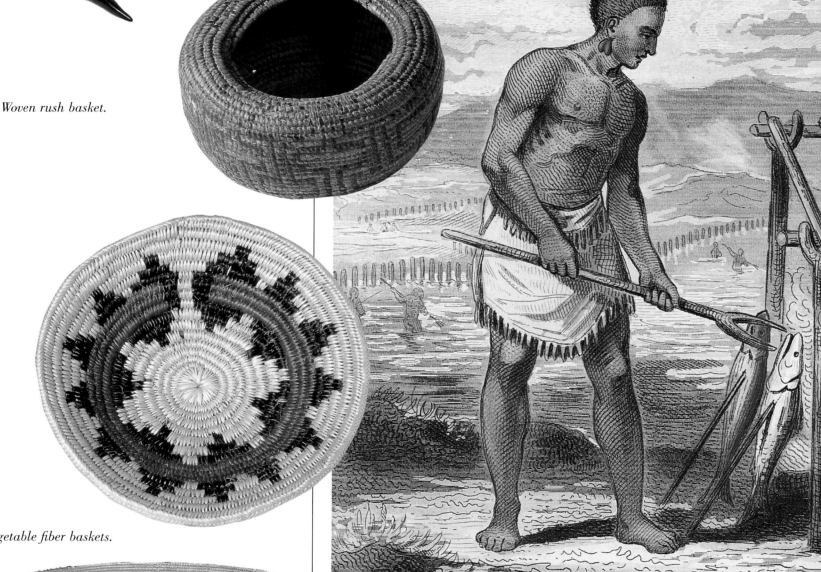

Vegetable fiber baskets.

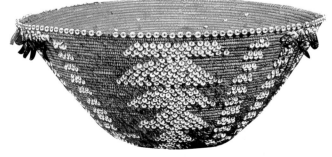

food and your host watched closely. He was there to ensure that the service you received was acceptable. Highly attentive and respectful, the host of the house even lit your pipe for you at the end of the meal. Now that's Indian hospitality!

Those Native Americans least vulnerable to famine practiced a combination of gathering, agriculture, hunting, and fishing. In this way they increased their chances of survival. In the Southwest, isolated on unproductive lands, in deserts where big game rarely ventured, Oodham Indians encountered more difficulties in feeding themselves than the worshippers of Ma-ni-too in the North.

Thanks to their bark canoes, many woodland Indians obtained

PEMMICAN

Indians who were obliged to make long journeys, especially those who lived by hunting, invented an exceptionally useful food called pemmican. To make it, women reduced the flesh of fish, elk or bison to a powder. Rich in protein, these powders were combined with bear marrow and with berries. After mixing this laboriously by hand, the woman obtained a thick paste that she poured into the bladder of the bear from which she had obtained the marrow. Tightly sealed, this "foodbox" was not affected by bad weather and preserved the food almost indefinitely. A trapper could subsist for many days on a ball of pemmican about the size of a fist, so great were its energy-providing powers.

Horn spoon.

Jewel box with its lid decorated

Wooden platter.

abundant supplies of fish from rivers and lakes. Good fishermen, they and other tribes used large vegetable fiber nets, hoop nets, and landing nets, and cast with hook and line. But some tribes in all areas occasionally lived from one day to another due to an unreliable and scanty food supply.

BISON AND WILD BERRIES

The carnivorous Plains Indians also consumed fresh vegetables and berries. Most historical Great Plains tribes came from the Great Lakes region, migrating west mainly during the 18th century. Their original territory was interspersed with rivers and wooded hills. These people fished in the rivers and hunted for deer, bear, and elk. They also trapped small mammals like beaver and otter, gathered berries and other wild plant foods, and ate fowl. Some

groups also gathered wild rice. Some cultivated many varieties of beans, maize, and squash. The diet of the Plains Indians consisted of around 60% meat, 10% fish, 20% wild vegetables, and 10% fruit. For some of the Lakes tribes, this was 50% maize (around one pound a day), 15% beans and sunflower seeds, 15% squash, 10% fish, 5% meat, 5% berries, nuts, leafy vegetables and maple syrup.

Harvests and Hunts

Many Indian peoples cultivated maize, beans, and squash, but agriculture depended on weather conditions, and the tribes often had to endure scarcity, or even famine.

In the central plains, hunters followed the bison. Neither farmers nor fishermen, they were reliant on the continual movement of wild game. The Dakota regarded cultivation of the ground as an insult to the Great Spirit since it allowed them to build up reserves of food that were incompatible with natural generosity. With rare exceptions, such as at grand banquets, Indians ate sparingly, at most once or twice a day. However, providing food became harder when a hunter had three or four wives and numerous offspring to feed.

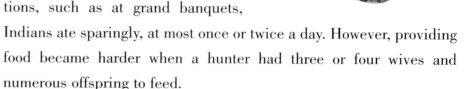

Indians taught the first colonists to grow maize, to cook clams, and to bury beans in a hole filled with embers and dig them up the next morning, ready cooked and delicious. Many people still enjoy skillfully cooked dishes like hominy and succotash.

A Favorite Dish

If, on arriving at a Plains Indian village, a dog ran between your legs, you could look forward to tasting it at the welcoming feast, boiled and served in your honor. To cook a dog was a way of showing one's friendship toward a visitor. Among some Indians, dog was a popular dish, eaten especially on ceremonial occasions. And if by chance the white man did not appreciate the tasty meal, the Sioux, far from being annoyed, concluded that the palate of the Paleface could not be as discerning as that of an Indian.

When the Potawatomis had some leisure time, men played lacrosse and the ring game. In the latter, they proved their agility, speed, and dexterity by being the first to catch a ring on the end of a long pole. Women played various ball and dice games.

A Plains Indian legend tells that the white bison was sent to earth by the Great Spirit, and was immortal. Men always spared it on their hunts. Ta-tan-ka was endowed with such supernatural powers that the great sorcerers gave themselves the title, Wa-sik-us-Ta-tan-ka, or Sacred White Bison.

TA-TAN-KA

The bison was indispensable to the lives of Plains Indians. The people used it for all their basic needs. In the hunting season, both men and women worked ceaselessly, accumulating reserves for the Season When the Snow Comes Into the Tepees. Throughout the summer, women cut bison joints into half-inch-thick strips, keeping a layer of fat on one side. These thousands of strips of meat dried in the sun in a few days. The flesh, dried in this way, was eaten throughout the year. But all parts of the bison were used: the skin for clothes and tepees, the horns for arrowheads and knife handles, the sinews for sewing thread, and the hooves for making glue. Before 1800, several million bison roamed the Great Prairies. With the arrival of non-natives, some of whom killed the animal purely for sport, and of the Iron Road (the train), nearly the entire species was wiped out. Today there are a few thousand head in Canada and the United States.

The Bison

Plains Indians obtained most of their resources from bison, and while fresh meat was eaten in the hunting season, women knew how to preserve it for the season of great cold. To prepare for hard times, they sliced the meat into thin strips, then dried them in the sun

on racks. After a week the dried strips of meat could be stored until needed. In winter, women soaked them to make them soft before cooking them in a stew.

Dakota Indians thought that the Great Spirit had created bison for the Indians and the very idea that the animal could one day disappear never occurred to them. But the whites understood that if they wiped out the bison, Plains Indians would not survive. The day of reckoning arrived when General Sheridan uttered his infamous slogan, "No more bisons, no more Indians!" One greedy man, Colonel William Cody, killed 5,000 bisons single-handedly in seven months: he was

nicknamed Buffalo Bill. General Phil Sheridan announced later, "The bison hunters have done more in two years for the solution of the Indian problem than the army did in ten." So the Plains Indians took the warpath not for pleasure but from necessity. The war cries of the proud Dakota were mingled with those of the Cheyenne, the Crow, the Comanche, and other tribes. The open spaces rang with vengeful cries of Hoka-Hey and You-You!

In the West, around 1800, a non-native claimed to have seen a herd of bisons that took five days to pass, and which stretched for four miles from one side to the other. This man was not mistaken: the bisons were virtually innumerable. In those days, there were more of them than there were people on the vast plains. Despite this abundance, the Indian did not kill more than he could use. Hunting was practiced by close approach and, after the people acquired horses, by pursuit. Sometimes hunters would also drive herds off cliffs.

To approach on foot, the secret was to trick the bison by taking on its own smell. The hunter covered his skin in bison fat so as not to alarm the animal. Armed with his silent bow and as many arrows as the number of beasts he wished to kill, he covered himself with a bison skin and, bent over, moving on his knees, he approached the herd and moved in among the animals. Under his camouflage, the Indian observed the beasts and made his choice. Avoiding the calves and females, he shot his arrows at the hollow beneath the shoulder. It was

In hunting as in war, Indians used bows and arrows. Other weapons included ball-headed war clubs, spears, knives and tomahawks. Some groups also used the last two weapons to remove scalps, a practice that Indians may have learned from early Spanish explorers. Both Indians and non-natives freely engaged in scalping. With the arrival of the non-natives Indians traded for tools and weapons with steel blades.

Hunting in Winter

In the Iroquois tribes who dwelt on the left bank of the Saint Lawrence River in Canada, there was often a shortage of meat. To ensure their survival, the Iroquois hunted even during winter. This practice was facilitated by an abundant snow fall. The animals left deep tracks and got stuck, while the hunter, equipped with his snowshoes, could move easily over the thick layer of snow.

imperative that the arrow went straight to the heart and that the bison fell stone dead. A missed shot meant a badly wounded male, a groan of pain, and great danger for the hunter. When he had killed the required number of animals, the hunter slipped away from the herd and frightened the beasts, who fled at a gallop. All that was left on the grass were the corpses.

Hunting on horseback was carried out in a different way, but was also dangerous, Here there were no tricks, it was simply a question of skill. Men, armed with bows and spears and mounted on swift, sturdy ponies, appeared on the edge of the herd. Their strategy consisted of frightening the animals with loud cries to make them turn around so that those at the head joined those at the rear to form a circle. In this gigantic vortex the males bellowed and hooves churned up the ground. The rout made such a racket that it sounded like thunder rolling. The noise could be heard miles away. Galloping at the edge of the herd, the Indian let go of his horse's bridle. Guided only by the rider's knees, the well-trained pony performed faultlessly. Arriving close to a large

male bull, the Indian slowed down, aimed, and shot. The arrow lodged in the shoulder. When the animal collapsed, the horse instinctively jumped aside and moved on to another without removing itself from the wild dance. When the Indian had no more arrows in his quiver, he continued his deadly chase around the herd with his spear. Accidents where a bison fell and crushed the horseman were invariably fatal. At the end of the hunt, the Indians sometimes had to wait a long time for the herd to move away. And if there were some hunters missing at the roll-call, the others would sing their praises at the camp fire in the evening. Death was a common enough occurrence for the courageous hunters.

THE MAN OF THE FOREST

Bear hunting took place before the animal went into hibernation, at a time when it still possessed all of its fat. To attack this formidable quarry was not without risks, and the hunter often paid the price of his temerity. The bear was hunted in two ways, on foot or on horseback, but so highly was the Man Of The Forest respected that hunters always followed an exact ritual. For the Indian, it had to be a "clean" fight, a struggle in which everyone stood a chance. As a challenge, the hunter explained to the animal beforehand that he needed its flesh to eat and its skin to clothe himself. The man who emerged victorious from this terrible combat placed a pinch of tobacco on the tongue of his adversary so that the latter could smoke along the path to the Land of the Brave Bears.

THE CANOE

To make a birch bark canoe, the Mohicans planted stakes in the ground in two straight lines that served as an external template.

Arches of ash wood were fixed every foot or so between the posts. Then they were linked together to form the two sides. These most practical of boats could travel equally well in both directions and were as useful in trade as in war.

Once built, the frame was covered with caribou skin or with birch bark, depending on the materials available at hand.

In both cases, the hull was held together with animal gut. Gluing and waterproofing were done with spruce-tree resin, which hardened in the sun. This glue or varnish gave the structure its required rigidity.

When finished, the canoe was painted and its two raised prows were adorned with the builder's clan totem, generally the image of its protector animal.

Boats

At the time of the wars between the French and the English, some members of the great Iroquois family lived scattered in small clans on the banks of the Saint Lawrence River and Lakes Erie and Ontario. Fishermen for millenia, they possessed a mode of transport suited to their needs: the canoe.

This boat met a variety of specifications: it could carry between ten and twenty people, was light enough that two men could carry it, was strong enough to shoot the rapids, and was constructed in such a way that it was easy and quick to repair anywhere, with birch bark and spruce resin.

In addition, when they attacked small forts or fortified villages, the Indians could lean their canoes against the palisades and use them as ladders: the crosswise wooden struts that served as benches for the paddlers doubled as rungs. The cleverly constructed canoe turned out to be a functional and multi-purpose item.

In this light and maneuverable boat, the Indian descended rapids like an arrow, riding the most turbulent chutes. When by some misfortune a hole was torn in the hull, wherever he was he could find the wood, resin, skin, or bark that he needed for repairs.

The Virginia, Powhatans, and the Delawares on the banks of the Ohio and the Potomac caught fish, but did not have extensive river systems like those in the Northwest. Neither did they have the proper materials to make bark canoes.

Their simple boats were more like dugouts, constructed from hollow trees. The great weight of these craft made them difficult to carry, so they were only used locally. These unstable and crude boats were not painted.

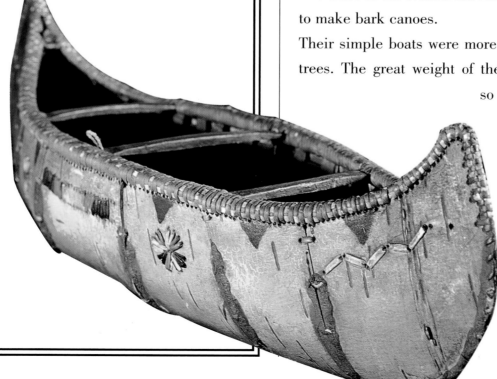

While Indians of the plains used horses as an important means of transportation, other Native Americans navigated lakes, rivers, and streams in bark and dugout canoes.

In Southwestern Canada, on the coast of British Columbia overlooking Vancouver Island, lived the Haida, the Totem Carvers. These people created gigantic "ships" that could contain fifty or a hundred braves, or even an entire village. To build these giants, they put together planks of red cedar 71 feet long in true shipyards. These coastal constructions could have one or two decks. Above the upper deck, a sort of dais held the tribal dignitaries. These aquatic giants, painted

in bright rainbow colors from the keel up to the totem on the prow, and which contained twenty-odd rowers, were not intended for fishing but for "tourism." The Haida visited friendly peoples to show off their splendor. They did not go by unnoticed: musicians beat time on huge drums, to accompany the flutists on board. On hearing this cacophony, the people would cry, "The Fire of Heaven is here!"

Every group of rowers possessed its own paddles, painted in its own colors. If the canoe unfortunately capsized, each rower could thus easily recover his own.

The Haidas of the Pacific coast made giant canoes from the trunks of red cedar. These vessels, whose raised prow was always carved into an effigy of a clan's animal totem, could brave the assaults of ocean waves without damage.

The Ka-O-W'at

For their part, the Mandans used a versatile craft called a bull-boat. Notwithstanding its practicality, some non-natives declared that they could not tell if these Indians took their baths in their boats or went boating in their baths. The bull-boat was constructed with a light framework and a bison skin hull.

It measured about 8 feet in diameter by a height of roughly 20 inches.

The sedentary Mandans lived principally on the banks of the Missouri. They lived in round lodges (wooden frames covered with earth), and banded together to form large villages. They were excellent navigators, and had invented an astonishing boat which was easy to carry, called the Ka-O-W'at, these round dinghies made from leather covering a wooden framework, allowed the Mandans to navigate the rivers and small watercourses.

Although inherently unstable, Mandans used it perfectly, mainly to cross bodies of water. Thanks to its light weight, an Indian fisherman could easily carry his boat on his back. His children could fill it with water and wash in it. When a storm approached, he placed this "giant umbrella" on the roof of his dwelling so that the water would not come in through the smoke hole. He also used it for storing berries and grain.

Commerce and Barter

Like all societies that lack a currency, the Indians made use of barter in their transactions. Merchandise was valued according to its use to the purchaser or as an item that might be re-traded for something else.

Many indians were skilled traders. Among themselves they might exchange furs, crops, shells, pipes, and feathers. From non-natives they imported metal tools, cloth, glass beads, and firearms. Whatever the price of the object to be traded, it always gave rise to interminable discussions.

When the sound of the great Talking Drums was heard across rivers and mountains, Indians traveled great distances to conduct trade.

In 1765, a French trader called Gregoire Delachapelle found, right in the middle of the Great Plains, a Dakota man carrying a whalebone bow. The Indian had traded for it with a Tlingit who lived surrounded by ice in the north of Canada, 2,000 miles away. Indians looked forward to trading with non-natives. The latter always brought an array of objects that were indispensable in the eyes of the Indian: multicolored beads, iron pots, metal knives, bowler hats and a variety of trinkets.

The non-native trapper visited Indian villages regularly to buy pelts that he could sell to his fur company. Indians often liked spending time with the trappers because they shared their simple lifestyle.

Sometimes the white man went away leaving behind his gun, his powder, and his bullets with an Indian who drove a particularly hard bargain.

Often, non-natives plied the Indians with alcohol in order to "loosen them up" for trade. Indians regularly asked the non-native authorities—in vain—to stop the illegal trade in liquor. Fire

THE HUDSON BAY COMPANY

Among other items, the Hudson Bay Company imported English blankets that some Indians were very fond of. This company had found a clever way of differentiating between the different qualities of blankets available. According to the selling price, the blankets bore one, two, three, or four small black lines, printed in a corner, which showed if the blanket was of cotton, wool and cotton, or pure wool. These lines corresponded with the number of skins that the tellers had to receive in exchange for one of them. These symbols took on a great importance in the Indian trade: when a native had a coat made out of one of these luxury items, he ensured that the renowned stripes were visible. Three or four symbols showed off the quality of his article. Such blankets are still made traditionally in England, and the black lines still indicate their quality.

Water too often gave rise to brawls and reckless exchanges. When the Indian had sobered up, all he had left were his eyes to cry with. Trade indicated the relative worth of things. An Indian might offer three horses for a simple pocket mirror, if it particularly caught his fancy. On the other hand, he could demand three guns for an otter skin, and refuse to budge if the otter was his medicine animal.

After the creation of the Hudson Bay Trading Company in 1670, larger numbers of Indians traded with the whites in Canada. They might travel for hundreds of miles to arrive at the trading post. They braved winds and storms bent down under the weight of rolls of skins of red fox, white wolf, and winter-coated beavers.

Later, the Yankees founded the Missouri Fur Company and the American Fur Company, decreasing the distance required to travel to a trading post, yet introducing more non-natives into Indian territory. Trade even occurred between enemy tribes — there were regular truces during which exchange took place. One tribe, with abundant stocks of dried meat, could come to the aid of its enemy by exchanging with them whatever they needed to get through the Sad Season without dying of hunger. Verbal credit arrangements allowed considerable flexibility: if the needy tribe had nothing to offer in exchange for the food, it was agreed that they would pay later, when they had become richer. In this case, the debtor group did not attack its creditor for as long as the debt was outstanding. Custom dictated that one felt grateful to one's benefactors.

Of course, the Indians were not always happy in their transactions with non-natives. In 1895, a Navaho weaver mistakenly traded the blanket she had just made for a few dollars at a trading post in New Mexico. Later, the same work of art was sold in a New York store for a tidy sum. Needless to say, the Navaho woman never received the difference!

THE TRADING POSTS

Trading post merchants, who were representatives of their companies, initially set themselves up in the army's forts. Throughout the year, Indians could find, in a fixed spot, a practical place for trade, set up by capitalist organizations. But these trading posts were often the scene of risky encounters. When by chance Comanches and Cheyennes came to sell skins at the same time, prudent soldiers disarmed the visitors at the fort's entrance, and the transactions took place peacefully. As killing each other was impossible, the Cheyennes and Comanches exchanged smiles, awaiting a more dramatic encounter.

Fort Laramie, at first an exchange center for Indian hunters, was purchased in 1836 by the American Fur Company to encourage trade in skins.

The pony, a new discovery...

The non-native says that the horse is our most beautiful conquest.

The Indian says that the pony is our best friend. The introduction of the horse,

mainly in the 17th and 18th centuries, was to completely change the daily life of many Indian

groups, especially those living on and near the Great Plains. The familiar animal also

became a currency for barter and, in certain tribes, it was a sign of wealth and grandeur.

Plains Indians organizing races. Victory belonged to the most skillful horseman, and to his fiery horse.

For parades, the horses wore embroidered decorations on their necks.

The Horse

Some Indians—for example, the Palouse—developed their own breed of horse. Many were among the best riders the world has ever known. To explain their failure to catch mounted Indians, non-natives provided a thousand excuses. Either the saddled mounts were heavier than those of the Indians, or the American cavalry were pulling cannons while the Indians could move unfettered. Not one of these reasons was valid. It was simply the case that the hunted possessed better horses—and generally more skill—than the hunters.

Indians lived close to the wild horses called mustangs. By observing the herd they came to know every animal, witnessed their births from a distance and noticed the exceptional qualities of a foal very quickly. Selection was made by watching an animal grow up and observing it closely, often for more than a year. When the pony reached an age when it could be ridden, the Indian captured him, and no other. Always in a hurry, non-natives often took all the horses they found and only made choices afterward.

Plains Indians preferred short, sturdy ponies, with piebald or spotted coats. These swift and hardy horses offered the additional advantage of having a very effective natural camouflage. They were much less visible than the tall black or brown horses of the U.S. soldiers.

As is true of many expert riders, Indians often felt they understood their horses. Many Plains Indians lived, so to speak, on their ponies, and when they dismounted the pony followed them right home. Among the Mandans, as with other tribes, man and beast slept in the same room.

The horse took part in many festivities and fully appreciated the honor that was paid to it. Others believed that the horse could not understand human speech, but Indians knew what was possible with patient training.

When he judged that he owed a victory to his brave pony, the Crow would offer it the Feather of Honor that the elders had just presented to him. It was added to the scalps that already hung from its mane.

By selective breeding, the Nez-Percés of Washington Wallowa Valley created a breed famous for its purity of proportion, its speed, its stamina, its bravery, and also for its spotted white coat. Today, one of their breeds, the Appaloosa, is so admired by horse experts that it is the focus of a lucrative trade.

On the East coast, the Na-ra-gan-set gave their name to a similar

NEW MOUNTS

Long before the conquistadors set foot upon the lands of the New World, huge herds of wild horses, descended from an indigenous breed, already lived on the vast prairies. However, the Redskins also valued the purebreds brought by the Spanish and lost no time in stealing large herds. The new mounts were immediately trained for hunting and for battle.

breed. In a distant past, the white colonists paid in gold for these even-tempered and sturdy horses, which were capable of crossing the unending plains and escaping from hostile tribes.

Very quickly, the horse became indispensable. Many tribes, such as

With the arrival of the Spaniards, the southern tribes learned to put saddles on their horses' backs, whilst those of the north continued to ride bareback.

Carved from a piece of turquoise — a symbol of abundance among the Hopis and Navahos — this figurine is a religious object. The pony was the Redskin hunter and warrior's most loyal accomplice.

the Comanche, undertook expeditions to steal those of their enemies. A Dakota or a Comanche trained his horse so well that it became one with him. The animal became an accomplice in his skill and picked up his patience, his recklessness, and his impetuosity. Responding to a simple squeeze of the legs, the horse would lie down on its side: horse and rider thus became invisible in the long grass. Once the danger had passed, the horse got up again without unseating the rider. A warrior lying flat along his horse covered long distances to give his

THE TRAVOIS

Before the introduction of the horse, dogs pulled the loads when Indians migrated. As Native Americans did not possess the wheel, Plains groups carried their belongings on a travois made of tepee poles. This V-shaped structure was tied together with leather thongs and placed over a dog's neck. Sticks fixed at right angles prevented them from moving apart and reinforced the structure.

Young children and the elderly sat among the baggage. As dogs could not carry heavy burdens, progress was slow and tiresome. During long winter marches, dogs got stuck in the snow and mud and slowed down the entire tribe. Horses made the migrations easier, and above all, quicker.

enemies the impression that a wild herd was passing. With the rider clinging to its side in this way, the animal managed not to alter its natural gait and aroused no suspicion.

Every warrior or hunter used a distinctive sound to call his horse. At

this signal, the horse came to him very naturally, without attracting an enemy's attention. The Indian's unshakable patience and his love of animals enabled him to obtain such results.

The Indians roused their horses by letting out a loud cry. The whip never made contact with an animal's sides. Riders cracked it in the air to encourage their mounts.

He Who Goes To Capture A Horse

Around the age of fourteen, a young Indian of the Plains went off to capture his first mustang. If he succeeded alone, he was given a proud name; but if he returned empty-handed he was forced to endure the worst ridicule. Before setting off, he paid a visit to the peace chief, who consulted the sorcerer to examine his chances. He restlessly walked to and fro among his people, puffing out his chest and already inspiring respect. Little by little he became He Who Goes To Capture A Horse. He went to purify himself in the river and to meditate in the sweat lodge, where he stayed for three suns without food, perspiring, and eliminating all bad spirits through the pores of his skin. Dreams and visions came to him there. The sorcerer interpreted them in the ashes of the fire and by casting the knucklebones. If the signs were favorable, the young man painted lightning flashes on his body to give himself speed, and drew a ray of the sun on his forehead to illuminate his path.

So that he could be agile and light, he took off his moccasins and fixed a jay's feather in his hair. Carrying no weapons, the young man slung his medicine bag across his shoulders and tied a rope that he had woven himself around his waist (this would be used as a bridle). Around his neck hung a bison's bladder containing five or six handfuls of pemmican. Thus prepared, he announced his departure to the whole tribe and set off at a run. His entire success depended on this long easy stride that would quickly become automatic. After twelve hours of exertion, his muscles were in agony. But if he stopped, even for an instant, he would not be able to go on and would become He Who Failed. The hunter suffered in silence. After twenty hours, his legs no longer ached, he moved on automatic, guided by his single motivation. Stretched out on his stomach, he drank from the streams without ever crouching down, and as he passed, he grabbed berries and fished for pinches of pemmican in his bison bladder. Suddenly, the herd he desired appeared before his misty eyes. Having attained his first goal, he could now rest.

The young man, hidden from sight and downwind of the horses, remained crouched behind a thicket. Lying on the ground, he massaged his legs and relaxed without ceasing to observe the herd. With his keen gaze, he had picked out a small piebald horse. The Indian knew that the only thing keeping himself from the horse was merely a need to wear the animal down.

Standing up, the young hunter began his loping run again and headed straight for the horse he had chosen. Immediately the herd fled, but the young man continued on

his path, keeping his rhythm and heading for the mustang. This exercise lasted a whole night. In the morning, the horses were no more than 150 feet away. As incredible as it may seem, the horse was less accustomed to the prolonged effort than the person. The young man knew this and took advantage of it.

When the leader of the herd felt that one of its number was being targeted, a few old males chased away the coveted animal. The Indian approached it to let it get used to his presence. When the horse stopped, the young man did the same. As soon as it set off again, the teenager followed it. During these countless stops, the Indian rested and ate while the mustang used up the last of its strength.

At last, the hunter slipped to within 30 feet of his future mount, spoke softly to it, advancing always closer, until he could offer his new friend a handful of fresh grass. The hungry horse accepted the offering. The Indian took the opportunity to stroke it furtively. If the frightened horse shied away and fled, the young man did not chase it, but rejoined it slowly, talking to it and offering it grass. With enough patience, he could touch the animal and make it eat out of his hand, so that the animal ended up following him.

The Indian put his arms around the horse's neck and murmured soothing chants into its ears. He blew into its nostrils so it could get used to his scent. He unwound the rope that he wore around his waist and tied it around the lower jaw of the horse. Then he slipped onto the animal's back, allowing himself to slide to the other side, and repeated this one minute later. The horse took this for a game and ended up accepting its rider. The capture was complete!

The young Indian returned to the camp on his horse and related his exploits to the elders. He had become a man and could paint on his shield the mark of He Who Possesses A Horse.

Indian garb

When the temperature permitted, many Indians lived almost naked; when cold bit, they donned appropriate garments. Clothing, richly decorated with embroideries or porcupine quills took on a great importance at councils, ceremonies, festivals… or when someone felt the need to put on a show so that others would admire him!

Some Indians competed with each other in elegance. When a Dakota met a group of Crows, he decked himself out with clothes that were representative of his tribe, such as, for example, a collar of bear claws.

From Top to Toe

In 1736, in a Boston saloon, a man returning from the West told his friends, "The Dakota woman is so skilled at working skins that the clothes she makes are the most beautiful you could ever see. The treated skins have the pliability of silk, the whiteness of snow and the feel of velvet." The man was not mistaken.

With knowledge gained from long practice, a woman first skinned an animal that a hunter brought her. She slit the skin around its circumference and pegged it out on the ground, or stretched it on a wooden rack kept for this purpose. After the drying process, the woman removed the hair from the skin, leaving only the core of the material. She then rubbed it thoroughly with brains and other material. A small tepee was reserved for curing. A fire of wood and carefully chosen herbs burned slowly and gave off large amounts of smoke. This penetrated the skin and helped make it waterproof. At this point, the skin was supple and impermeable, even in a torrential downpour. In some tribes, the woman obtained an incomparable pliability by patiently chewing the skin, inch by inch. An Indian's usual clothing comprised a breechclout and possibly a shirt or a pair of leggings for the man, a skirt or dress for the woman, and moccasins. The moccasin was extremely functional, warm in winter and cool in summer, and it demanded great skill in its manufacture. It was cut from a single piece of skin and contained only one stitch.

The sole resisted water. The high moccasins of the Hopis and Navahos resembled boots: they covered the calves and took the place of leggings.

Some Apaches took the whole skin from a deer's leg without tearing it and, after an initial treatment, put it on. After a second treatment, it molded itself to the shape of the Apache's foot. These moccasins were the envy of enemy tribes.

People pulled leggings, or "mitas," up to the top of the thighs and attached them to the waist with leather straps. They never wore anything under a shirt or skirt, but in the bitter Sad Season, they wrapped themselves in a luxurious warm bison skin, with the fleece on the inside. With a bone needle, a woman sewed clothing with very small stitches, using the sinews of elk, bison, or antelope. Once the piece was finished, it was time to think about embroidery, which could be colorful, bright, and lavish. Embroidered designs told of the life and the victories of the wearer, or the history of the tribe, or they might simply be decorative.

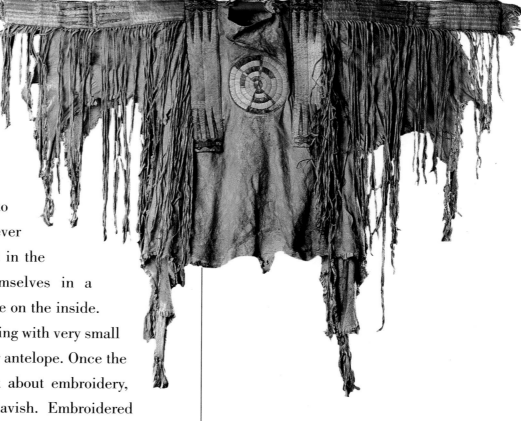

Pieces of skin were fitted by a clever interlacing of fringes at the seams.

Scraper used to remove impurities from the skin.

An Iroquois man's moccasins, embroidered with colored glass beads.

Some Apache warriors wore supple buckskin or antelope skin boots, decorated with silver studs.

The Iroquois most often depicted snow-flakes, plants, and flowers in a stylized form. The Dakota preferred images of sunrays, the shapes of tepees, and flowing streams.

To keep out the winter cold, men and women of the tribes of northern Canada wore fur snowsuits, decorated with symbols designed to keep away evil spirits.

Hat made from sea-otter skin, worn by dignitaries on Vancouver Island.

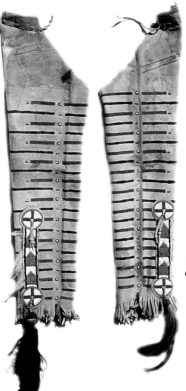

Deerskin leggings, decorated with simple paintings in walnut dye, with scalps hanging at the ends.

Jewels and Ornaments

Before the appearance of glass jewelry, Indian women embroidered with porcupine quills that had been specially softened. Originally, beads were carefully cut by hand from the insides of sea shells. These mollusks were carried into the plains after being exchanged many times between tribes. Only the middle of the shell could be used to make round red beads. From the thickest part, women extracted an elongated bead. The hole was made using a bone needle dipped in fine sand. Then the beads were polished by hand. When non-natives arrived with large quantities of pre-made, multicolored beads, native bead manufacture slowly began to decline. Indians greatly valued these and other non-native items and sometimes paid dearly to acquire them. Imagine the astonishment of a traveling salesman who was offered a horse in exchange for the twenty thimbles in his pack. The white man thought that the wife of this Indian must be very hard working, but the following year when he passed the same way, he was once more relieved of all his thimbles. When the friendly Indian invited him into his tepee, the stunned man saw his host's wife proudly wearing a dress decorated with the first batch of thimbles that he had traded, the

The Sauk chief Ap-pa-noo-se.

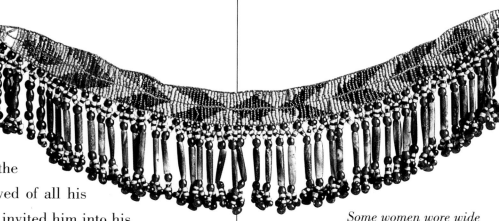

Some women wore wide necklaces. Glass jewelry, shells and multicolored beads are arranged in decorative, clan, or spirit motifs.

FEATHERS FOR THE WARRIORS

Before the arrival of the non-natives, Indians made use of materials ideally suited to their way of life. Indians did not generally wash their clothes, preferring to wait until they fell to pieces. Garments of non-native manufacture often brought more problems than advantages. Well-worn leather keeps all its useful properties, while wool or cloth, dirty with sweat, grease and germs, gradually loses them.

The Dakota "won" his great headdress of eagle feathers throughout his life. Victory in war, services rendered to his people, and acts of bravery earned a man an eagle's feather that was added to his collection.

All these feathers amounted to evidence of the strength, courage, daring, and kindness that he had shown over the years.

Thus attired in his ceremonial eagle's feather headdress, the Dakota man cut a fine figure!

bottoms of which had been pierced. The thimbles hung glittering on the dress like bells. The woman had started a fashion!

The wampum "belt," common in the Northeast, had nothing to do with clothing. In some tribes the word wampum means "story," for others, it means "agreement" or "treaty." The length of this leather band (the reason why it is called a belt), varied according to what an Indian wanted to say. Wampum was often used to recount events or to formalize a treaty.

When two tribes, or a tribe and a non-native group, concluded an agreement, the Indians made a wampum on which they recorded the reasons for the decisions. The recipients hung it around their necks or wore it around their waists. When the Iroquois formed the Great League, a wampum was presented to the most important representatives of the assembly. The motifs showed five squares symbolizing the five houses of the five chiefs of the five nations. These squares were surrounded by images symbolizing complete accord.

After a peace treaty was concluded, numerous white generals found themselves presented with wampum belts showing broken arrows. With this sign, the Indians showed their peaceful intentions. During the wars for possession of Canada, the French General Montcalm received so many wampums that he, in his turn, had to have them made so that he would be taken seriously by his Huron allies.

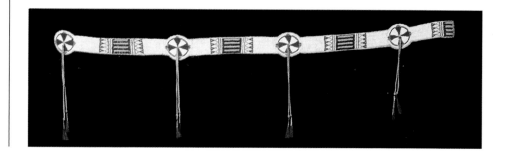

The Art of the Headddress

O n an elder, white hair evoked experience and wisdom. When an elder referred to his great age, he made allusions to the snow covering his white hair. In addition to the fine costumes of dances and ceremonies, traditional headdresses presented a great diversity of forms and appearances. Each tribe had its own styles. Everyday headdresses were simple, or not used at all.

On feast days, the Crow wore, flat on the top of his head, a decoration made of seven or eight feathers that were joined at a central point and spread out like the spokes of a wheel. The Fox represented her medicine totem with a pendant fixed on the nape of her neck: two jay's feathers pointing toward the sky to symbolize the ears of the animal. Cherokees adopted a small eagle's feather crown, while the Dakotas arranged the tail feathers of the same bird around a bonnet made from otter or marten. The Cheyenne allowed a lock of hair to fall over the left-cheek and attached an eagle's feather to it. As for the Apache, he contented himself with a cloth headband, preferably red, which he tied at the nape of his neck.

Osage Indians.

Headdress of porcupine quills; the eagle feather was added for ceremonies.

AN ORIGINAL HEADDRESS

The headdresses of some Plains Indian chiefs hung down to the waist. In warrior groups, they hung down as far as the heels. These decorations, won feather by feather in the course of one's life, were worn by deserving men at all ceremonies. The prestigious headdress was made up of tail feathers. The shaft of a feather, from which the barbs had been shaved, stuck up at the top of the headdress. This "antenna" pointing to the sky allowed the wearer to communicate more easily with the Eternal Being.

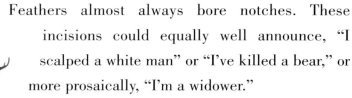

Feathers almost always bore notches. These incisions could equally well announce, "I scalped a white man" or "I've killed a bear," or more prosaically, "I'm a widower."

Nowadays, at the annual rodeo parades like those at Albuquerque and Calgary, those decorated with feathers ride by on their ponies before doing battle on the broncos (untameable horses) and wild bulls.

The Horned Headdress was the preserve of the sorcerers. It was a bonnet of valuable fur. Two bison horns jutted out from the front. The great Dakota leader Sitting Bull wore one that indicated his rank.

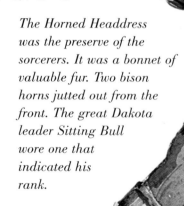

To Each his own Hairstyle!

As might be expected with a diverse people, different Indian groups wore different hairstyles. Cheyennes kept their hair long, divided into two plaits which hung down on each side of their faces. Hurons wore a "roach": a plume running from the forehead to the nape of the neck.

Iroquois men preferred to have the head shaved, except for a lock on the back of the head, called a Scalp Lock. Worn as a provocation, this lock meant, "Come and get it if you dare." Luckily there were very few who were willing to try such an affront! Some Dakotas liked to wear a fringe cut straight across the forehead, while Comanches had a tuft of hair brushed up on the top of their heads.

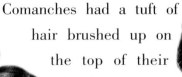

The quest for the Eternal Lands

Almost all Native Americans were deeply religious. They were also superstitious. Some honored a God or great Creator. Many people invoked a large number of spirits. In fact, among many groups, all animate and inanimate things were considered to have a spirit. Most Indians were profoundly aware of their proper place in the natural world.

At the cemetery of the Silent Ones, the snows whitened the bones of the people just as they stripped the flesh from the bisons' skulls...

The Thunderbird

In some Indian cultures, the Thunderbird, or Firebird, appears in the guise of a stylized eagle holding lightning flashes in its claws, or rising from the flames. Why this particular bird? We must look for the explanation in Indian mythology.

In the Rocky Mountains lies a peak called Thunder Nest. An eagle lays her eggs there with a terrifying noise. When the babies hatch, lightning flashes from the sky and a storm rages. This female is immortal, but cannot give life because the male, a serpent, kills the newborn chicks with his tongue. Many shamans have seen this bird, no bigger than the end of a finger. This legend also seems to be the origin of the Apaches' Feathered Serpent.

The United States government put the eagle on its crest; the inspiration for this may have been the famous Thunderbird of the Indians.

During religious dances some apprentice shamans wore masks uniting the good and bad spirits.

Indian Gods

In 1886, when Goh-hla-yeh, the famous Chiricahua Apache chief Geronimo, was invited to Fort Davis to sign a peace treaty with the U.S., he listened to a missionary's sermon, visited the town and, among other places, the church. U.S. representatives thought that the Apache would be impressed by the power of the Christian God and would stay in the San Carlos reservation in Arizona. In fact, when he returned to his people, Geronimo said, "The whites are mad! They imagine that a divine being can agree to live in a dark, joyless square cabin. They have no God! We have one! We are the stronger ones!" The stagecoach that arrived the next morning brought bad news: the Chiricahua chief had withdrawn into the mountains. It took six generals and five thousand soldiers to subdue the famous warrior and his handful of men. Non-natives had a hard time understanding that Indians had their own legitimate ways of looking at things.

Like most Indians, Geronimo honored many spirits: Ga'an, or mountain spirits, were especially important to the Apache. Although there were similarities between them, the gods of each tribe bore different names. The Dakota venerated Wakan Tanka, the

Great Spirit, while the Iroquois worshipped Ma-ni-too, The Spirit of the Earth. The Zuni called their gods A-wo-na-wi-lo-na, the Sky Being, and his wife, H'u-ra-tu-a-tira, the Earth Mother. The god of the Pawnees was called Ti-ra-wa-a-tius, Father Sky or He Who Is Above. The Pueblos were protected by various Kat-chi-na, or Spirits, and practiced the cult of Ana-sa-zi, the Ancestors. The Assineboin listened to Wa-kon-la-la, the Voice of the Great Cloud Spirit, and it was with the help of Mi-de-wi-win, the Great Medicine, that the Anishinabe communicated with their protector. The Blackfeet feared the night because it was the time when Wa-pa-na-na, the Star Which Sets Behind The Mountain, could not see them. In Southern Alaska, the Goo-en-hoot, the Fugitives, drove away Hai'-mas, the Southern Squall, placing themselves under the protection of Kwu-kwu-ku-li-gye, the Thunderbird, the only one who gives access to Tem-larh'-am, the Promised Land.

To enable the benevolent gods to control the malevolent ones, to this day the Tlingit of Canada represent the two entities together on their totem poles. These Indians of the Far West acknowledge the superiority of the good gods over the evil ones, while other tribes think the opposite. The carvings on the totem poles also recount the history of the village, and it is often difficult for the uninitiated to distinguish the religious images from the events of war.

When the shaman wanted to emphasize his authority, he wore the horned bonnet, a sign of his supremacy over the other elders.

The Sorcerer

Nearly every Indian group possessed its sorcerers, or holy people. They knew all the medicine mysteries and possessed particularly strong spirit powers. Some possessed a whole panoply of items for telling the future. Their recipes were kept secret, and held the power of their medicine. Medicine men and women used and abused their privileges; they made the Sad Seasons and the Good Seasons. Was an attack planned? With one word the shaman could cancel the preparations by declaring that certain spirits did not favor the encounter. The war chief took care to make him his ally, to give himself elbow room. There was no question of digging up the war hatchet without the proper spiritual blessings.

Feared and dreaded, the shaman often succeeded by heredity to this thankless but coveted position. But one could also train as a medicine man if he had the right sort of dream. A reigning sorcerer was responsible for teaching the shamanic rites to the trainee.

In some tribes, a special hut allowed the sorcerer to go into seclusion. He devoted himself to uttering incantations to communicate with the spirits and predict the future. He lit fires and carefully observed the clouds of smoke for long periods; he threw a handful of twigs and read the geometric forms they made when they fell to the ground. He did the same with

Lighting the tobacco before a ceremony or a council was the shaman's duty. The peace pipes were very often kept in pairs. The medicine man saved one for his own use and invited those present to smoke the other.

pebbles or knucklebones, reading just as easily in the sand, the clouds, or the entrails of a frog. His conclusions could bring prosperity or lead to the worst calamity!

The Mystery of the Spirits

In 1737, by the McKenzie River, a French Catholic missionary was explaining to a Dené chief, who was himself called Supreme Man, all the blessings that God the Father could bring. The Dené reflected for a long time on the good priest's words and concluded, "Your god is good. He desires the happiness of all the Denés and we shall adopt him!" The happy priest responded, "Then assemble your people, we shall pray to your new God." "No," replied the Indian, "we would be wasting our time. It's the hunting season and our people are hungry. Your god is so good that it's pointless to devote time to him. He cannot harm us, so let's appease the evil spirits instead, because they could easily spoil the hunt." The missionary had not explained the Dené that the Catholic God could also be angry: Supreme Man had not understood that a god could be both good and bad at the same time.

Before the bears went into hibernation, the sorcerer dressed himself in a bearskin and armed himself with a spear: it was time to go hunting the Man of the Forest.

Most Indians recognize countless evil spirits. Among the most malevolent are Ya-woh-nik, the Serpent Who Is Never Satisfied; Ig-rak, the Bird Who Never Sleeps; Tsa-mak-qua, the Monster Who Never Moves. These dreadful spirits mostly live in Dai-swa-ga-ha, the Valley of the Skeletons, or come from the other side of Put-la-ga-muc-ka, the Stinking Water in the East, or the Atlantic Ocean.

The good spirits inhabit the infinite spaces of the Great Plains, the mountain tops and the beds of fast-flowing streams. When an Indian wishes to speak with his personal spirit she might draw a circle on the ground and sit inside it: only the benevolent gods can enter the circle.

Made from the skin of a small mammal, the medicine bag of the shaman, the tribe's healer, contained, along with his ritual objects, medicinal plants such as cinchona bark, sage, coca, and others known only to himself.

The Kat-chi-na

The sacred dolls represented the renowned supernatural forces of the Pueblos. The people invoked male Kat-chi-nas for decisions concerning wars, demarcation of hunting grounds, etc. Female spirits, for their part, enabled Hopi women to calm the destructive elements that caused famine, illness, and death.

Under a bunch of sage leaves, the shaman purified dolls that had been exposed to profane eyes for too long.

Medicine

The word "medicine" appeared with the first colonists. These people thought that the bag that some Indians wore contained herbs used for healing wounds and illnesses. It is more accurate to translate "medicine" as "mystery," or better, "magic."

Among some tribes, infants received a medicine bag at birth. It contained her soul along with her secret name. To lose one's bag amounted to losing one's soul and one's name. The child then faced a sad future, until she found another name and soul at the start of her adolescence.

At puberty, many Indians undertook a vision quest. This generally involved moving away from the tribe and fasting alone. For roughly three suns, a young person prayed in order to discover what his medicine would be. The first animal that was revealed to him became his guardian spirit. From that moment onward, the Indian could never again kill an animal of that species without destroying himself.

The medicine bag was always decorated. In some tribes, people possessed two medicine bags: one, secret and sealed, was never opened and was sewn into the clothing or worn next to the skin; the other was used as a satchel in which a person kept his pipe, his tobacco, his body paints and his talismans (bear claws, stones, feathers, hare's feet, certain herbs…). Both bags contained sacred objects.

Among those who followed the custom, medicine bags were their very life, and their protection.

An Indian could not get rid of her medicine: it formed part of the gifts bestowed on her by the Great Spirit. To sell the bag, give it away, lose it, or have it stolen condemned the unfortunate individual to becoming a Person Without Medicine, deprived of the respect of her people.

The Sweat Lodge

Many Indians based their actions on the interpretation of dreams and smoke clouds, the flight of birds, and the "other side." But it was above all his visions that dictated one's approach to life.

One way to achieve visions was in the sweat lodge, or steam bath. The sweat lodge was also used as a place of ritual purification and of simple recreation. The lodge was constructed differently depending on the tribe. Among the Plains Indians it was a small hide tent (a tepee) laid out in a special way. Among the Forest Indians, a cabin of branches (a wigwam) was used for the purpose.

THE MEDICINE BAG

Dakota medicine bag decorated with beads depicting the four cardinal directions. The metal motifs, cut out of shiny tin cans, show that it was made no earlier than the 18th century.

In both cases, a fire pit was dug in the ground at the center of the lodge; above this was placed an openwork basket. A fire was lit and covered with stones. When the stones were very hot they were drenched with water, which gave off large amounts of steam.

Sometimes a man might spend several suns in the sweat lodge. There, without eating or drinking, he perspired freely and stayed immobile until he entered an altered state. He passed out several times in this steamroom. When he came to, he interpreted the hallucinations he had experienced. If he was moved to announce that he had received a message, and if he was listened to, he might change the course of the tribe's existence.

These visions were the inspiration for war parties and major hunting expeditions; they could also cause a tribe to move camp and set up the village 200 miles away.

Before every war sortie, young Plains warriors prayed to the Good Spirits. They consulted the smoke clouds, messengers from the other side, and sought strength of the bison.

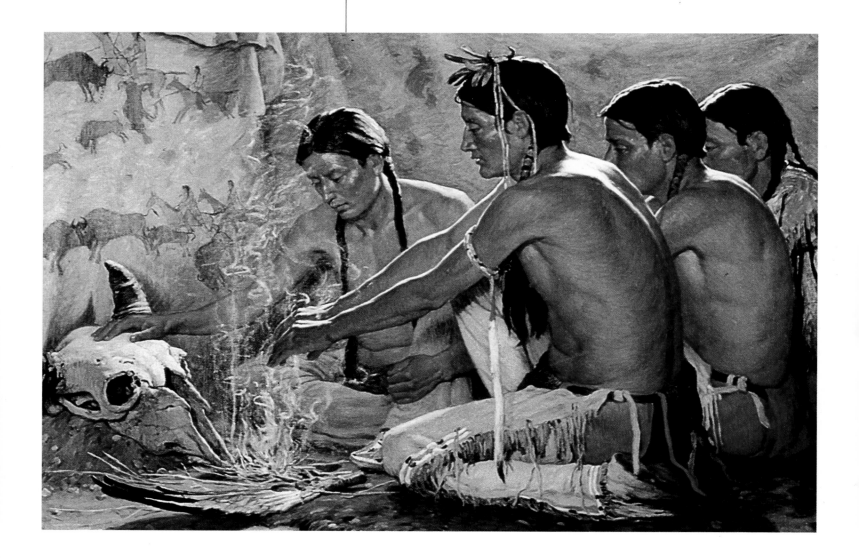

The Peace Pipe

One of the things most tribes held in common seems to have been the use of the peace pipe. The peace pipe must not be confused with an ordinary pipe. The latter was used for enjoyment by the men and women. The peace pipe was a precious object. It has been in use in North America for at least 4,000 years!

For the Dakota, the Cheyennes, the Comanches, the Pawnees, and other tribes, the bowl could only be obtained from a red stone quarry situated in a high place, called Tchan-dee-pah-sha-kah-free, Pipe Bowl Mountain. This mountain produced a soft stone called "pipestone" or catlinite, and was situated where the St. Peter River joined the Missouri. Many tribes extracted stone from it, and even if they were enemies, they observed a truce within its boundaries.

As legend has it, the Great Spirit sat down and rested in that place long ago. As he was hungry, he ate a bison; that is why the stones are red, the color of blood. Satisfied, the Great Spirit made with his hands the first peace pipe; raising it to the four cardinal points, he made it known that this stone was the flesh of all the Indians, that all must use it for making peace pipes to spread smoke across the earth in a message of peace.

The tribes gathered in the quarry, they burned K'-nick-K'-neck, tobacco, as an offering to their spirits, and asked their permission to take a piece of stone to make the precious pipe. Permission was always granted, and the Indians returned to their homes.

Before every ceremony or important discussion, or to prove to a visitor that they received him without aggressive thoughts, the peace chief lit the peace pipe at the council of elders and made everyone smoke it. By this act, he drew the attention of the Great Spirit to the group. The elders also knew that this custom allowed time for reflection. How many non-natives would have gained from practicing it....

Made from fine materials, the peace pipe was of a sacred nature. The stem of rare wood, horn, bone, or reeds, was laboriously carved, worked, and decorated.
Piercing the inner shaft required a great deal of care and skill, as the hole was created by friction with a bone or stone needle and fine sand.

Religious Customs

Indians paid homage to the spirits in numerous ways.

Thus, when a Nootkan from Vancouver Island announced his departure on a whale hunt, his wife threw herself down on her bed and started groaning. The poor woman twisted and turned, seeming to be afflicted with the most dreadful pains. As soon as her husband had captured the cetacean, his wife's suffering disappeared as if by a miracle. In reality, the hunter's wife was mimicking the suffering and death of the whale, killed by a harpoon. The end of her disturbing behavior corresponded to the departure of the marine mammal's soul for the peaceful land of the Eternal Being.

The Haidas of the West Coast, performed group dances in which the participants covered their faces with a mask. These artificial wooden faces, called "Changing Faces," could change their expression on command. Furnished with a clever mechanism, one only had to pull the cords of these masks to make them adopt different appearances. In this way they represented good or bad spirits without the need to change masks in the course of the ceremony.

"...Widow, your husband had avoided the Land of Shadows, now he will reside in the Eternal Hunting Grounds and the Great Spirit henceforth will watch over him..." The Guardian Spirits.

Let the party begin...

Most indian people had a great fondness for games of skill and chance. They also loved to gather together around a fire to relax and tell the myths and legends of their tribe.

Ball games might begin with men dancing around their team's goal while women pounded the ground in time. The sorcerers gathered at the center of the field.

On their signal, the men began to play, with no other goal than to gain victory for their side.

Games

Many pastimes could be divided into two general categories: games for profit and games for amusement.

The Ball Game

Among the Choctaws, the ballgame was an energetic entertainment. The contest began at dawn and continued until night time. A tribe severely beaten in combat by another wished to take its revenge.

The day before, the field was chosen and measured: a large rectangle with a goal constructed at each end from two poles ten paces apart, linked by a third placed horizontally about 12 feet above the ground. In the morning, the players assembled in their respective teams, holding in their hands a sort of long-handled wooden racket, the curved end of which held a net woven from strips of skin. The game was played with a leather ball as hard as wood. Today, we know this game as lacrosse.

The betting over, a referee placed the ball at the center of the field. At a signal from the sorcerers, the six or eight hundred gladiators threw themselves headlong into an infernal din. Each one tried to catch the ball in his crook to put it into the goal. All shouted, ran, jumped, and gesticulated, trying frantically to get hold of the ball. All possible means were allowed to achieve one's ends: catching others by the legs, knocking them out, hurling oneself on top of another, hitting and jostling each other. Groups formed and attacked other groups. Whole groups of players collapsed, covering the ball with a hundred sweaty bodies. A thick cloud of dust was thrown up and sometimes the ball was lost; a group searched for it on one side fighting their way through a chaotic melee, while the game continued elsewhere.

When a participant put the ball into the goal, he scored a point and

Two villages often competed against each other. The "combatants," their bodies painted in the colors of their team and their backs decorated with feathers symbolizing lightness and agility, opposed each other in a forceful encounter. Violence was often part of the "relaxation" and entertainment.

With a scowling face, it was necessary to impress, that is to say, intimidate, the opposition.
The reputation of the community was at stake, and there was no room for slacking.

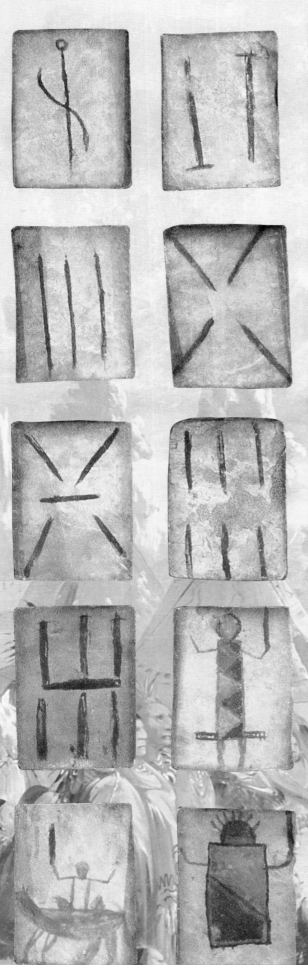

the sorcerers allowed a moment's respite. But as soon as the medicine man restarted the match, the tumult began again, more fierce, more bitter and more energetic.

According to the rules of the game, dangerous assaults were not allowed. However, by the end of the game, there were numerous minor injuries, serious wounds and even fatalities.

After such a turbulent encounter, players might spend a whole day sitting still, serenely smoking a pipe.

The Card Game

Inveterate players of games, Native Americans were fond of demonstrating their subtlety in numerous games of chance. To this effect, a tribe had invented a game of cards, consisting of rectangles of leather on which ideograms were etched. This game, whose rules were unclear to non-natives was the subject of large bets and sometimes lasted several days and nights.

The Faces Game

Perhaps the most mysterious game to outsiders was the Faces Game, which was often the pretext for outrageous bets with unfortunate consequences. Indians have lost their weapons, their dogs, even their spouses. Pat Holloway, an agent of the American Fur Company, describes the scene he witnessed:

"The sorcerer of the tribe, who also played the role of referee, distributed five small round pieces of stone to each of the players. After this, he explained to me that to succeed, the competitors must not only place the smallest possible number of pebbles on the ground, but must also describe the geometric face that they depicted. As night fell, the players sat down facing each other and immediately plunged deep into their thoughts to work out a strategy. According to the information I was given, each participant created his secret plan of action, an attack, a parry, a counter-attack, and when everyone declared themselves ready, the game could begin.

"Only at that point did the gamblers decide on a stake, and as the amount was unlimited, one bet almost his entire stock of fishing gear. The other, hoping to win, bet three stacks of rich furs, a quiver with its arrows, his great feather headdress, and two pairs of snowshoes, the most precious of his goods.

"The most fierce of the two was called Extra Pipe. He belonged to the Gros Ventre tribe that lived in Canada. Extra Pipe had traveled eight days to encounter his adversary, Trunk From The Top, an Iroquois of the Onondaga tribe known for his great clairvoyance and greed. While Extra Pipe watched him ferociously, Trunk From The Top focused himself one last time. Then, glaring at his associate with eyes that had become inhuman, he placed two stones on the ground and waited.

"It should be said here that it was incumbent on Extra Pipe to reveal the face represented by the arrangement of the stones, and as he said nothing, Trunk From The Top cried exultantly, 'Here is the elk, these pebbles are the two holes of his nostrils!' With the assent of the sorcerer, Trunk From The Top carried off the quiver, the arrows, the great headdress, and the snowshoes.

"This first win apparently gave him the advantage of going again. The Iroquois adopted a frightful grimace, threw his opponent a look full of venom, and placed a single stone on the ground that the sorcerer-referee had just cleared.

"Exactly like the first time, Extra Pipe held his head in his hands. His complexion turned pale when he heard Trunk From The Top announce: 'Here is the bear and this single stone is his nose!'"

The assembled crowd shouted enthusiastically, congratulated the winner and gave the loser a sound beating. He had just brought dishonor to his people.

Pat Holloway tried to get further information about the rules of the game and the order of play. But as he did not understand one word of the medicine man's explanations, he vowed never to challenge an Iroquois to play the Faces Game.

THE HIDDEN HAND

Brother Francis Duhamel, itinerant monk of the Brotherhood of Jesus, describes this game as he saw it among the Hurons:

"The Hidden Hand (or the Hand Game) is the great passion of the Indians of the North: the Algonquian Hurons, the Iroquois, and above all the Denés. The competitors place themselves in two lines facing each other, sitting side by side with their bodies touching. The hands, concealed under a blanket, touched each other, making hidden contact. One of the players held a knucklebone in one of his hands. It was for the opposition to work out which one. At a given signal, with the goal of throwing them off the scent, every arm and chest started moving. Bodies leaned across each other, shoulders were raised, bent forward and straightened up, bodies leaned back in jerks and spasms. Glaring at the opponents as if to paralyze them, one would say that their eyes were going to burst out of their sockets. The spectators, in a state of mass excitement, danced, waved their arms about, grimaced and yelled. Unbelievably quickly the 'leader' stopped the hullaballoo and indicated with an agreed gesture, imperceptible to the uninitiated, which one out of the ten or thirty hands contained the knucklebone. He made them open their hands at the same time to prove that there had been no cheating. If he was correct, the knucklebone and the game changed sides. If he was wrong, the victors started again with an even louder racket. The Castors (a band of the Ojibwa) spent whole days and nights in this way, making a furious row in the snow or in the rain. The game over, they collapsed in exhaustion."

Dancing was often of a religious nature for the Indian. It did not glorify a god but was connected with many ceremonies of prayer and hope. Dancing before a hunt might be concerned with casting out troublesome evil spirits. The dance often took the form of a mime: it showed the progress of the hunt, the difficulties encountered, and the final success.

The Dance of Secret Love Affairs

Among the Wichita, the Dance of Secret Love Affairs, also called the Womens' Great Confession, presented an entertaining spectacle. If on his return from hunting a man felt doubts about the fidelity of his wife, he might confide in the sorcerer. To settle the supplicant's uncertainty, the shaman consulted his magic, communed with the Great Spirit, and concluded that the dance of repentance could begin. As the news spread throughout the tribe, it aroused general curiosity and everyone joined in the preparations enthusiastically: women piled up wood, children collected presents while men smoked their pipes.

The appointed day arrived at last. The numerous inquisitive people sat themselves around the fire. The six-holed flutes played a happy tune, while great drums beat time enthusiastically. Then the sorcerer declared, "Women, Dance! Show us your lovers!"

When the general enthusiasm reached its highest point, women presented themselves one by one. Each one had to perform her own dance. The wives disguised themselves so as to resemble the man they had taken as a lover during the absence of their husband. They adopted his gait and his mannerisms so that the curious onlookers could easily recognize him. The unfortunate husbands laughed and joked with the lucky beneficiaries, for under no circumstances was this festival to create bitterness or resentment. When a

During one of their dances, the Comanches imitated the destructive elements. This dancer has placed strips of hide on the string of his bow to symbolize rain, the source of blessings but also of floods.

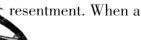

wife, covered with a deer skin, jumped over the fire, she made it known that she had transgressed with Agile Deer. Another, her dress stuffed with grass and her face covered by a two-horned mask, communicated that she had loved Fat Buffalo. Yet another, her naked body entirely covered with yellow paint and speckled with black spots, moved on her stomach along the ground: she had known Snake of the Rocks. As the music became frenetic, the sorcerer cried continuously, "Dance, our wives! Show us who takes our place in our absence!" As soon as the unfortunate husband recognized the lucky beneficiary, he went to congratulate him. The children gave them presents. The wayward wife was praised to the skies. Everyone commended her for her resourcefulness and her cunning mind. This festival lasted a whole night. The next day, the wronged husband forgot his own misfortunes by thinking of those of the others.

THE BISON DANCE

For the Bel-lohck-na-pic, the Bison Dance of the Oglala, the hunters gathered around the fire. They put animal skulls over their heads to imitate a herd. Some covered their bodies with a fur, others danced completely naked. This celebration formed part of a recurring cycle of events, like the annual departure for the Great Hunts. It was both a matter of entreating the good will of certain spirits and of miming the people's past problems so that they would not recur.

THE EAGLE DANCE

Although they differed from tribe to tribe, some groups adopted similar dances. This was the case with the Eagle Dance, for this bird of prey was found throughout almost the entire continent. To Indian eyes, it personified the Eternal Being because it flew higher than the other birds. The Eagle Dance was one of the most spectacular and the most enjoyable to watch. It narrated the capture of an eagle. In one version, the tribe assembled, sitting in a circle. Drums went into action, quickly accompanied by rattles. Singers began to wail. The rhythm became faster and suddenly, with an incredible leap, a man dressed as an eagle burst into the circle. The man, clothed in the bird's feathers, imitated its majestic and powerful flight.

Then the hunter appeared in his turn. He made the movements of stringing a bow and firing an arrow. The spectators kept their hands over their mouths throughout the death throes of the eagle. But then the sorcerer arrived, breathed into the bird's beak, and it came back to life. And if it didn't reach the heights, it was the fault of the dancer, who was unable to fly!

Before engaging in a punitive raid occasioned by the theft of some horses, the warriors of some tribes performed the Dance of Men Who Have Fallen Into Bad Ways. The aim of the expedition was not to claim victims. For this offense, it was enough to touch the transgressors with a coup stick to see them fall to the ground and play dead. The guilty party expiated his wrongdoing by laying still on the ground, alone with his thoughts of repentance.

THE RAIN DANCE

In the dry areas of New Mexico and Arizona, the farming Pueblos depended on rain. After a long drought, the people went to consult a sorcerer. When the medicine man, adorned with the symbols of his status, agreed to plead their cause, he collected the ingredients needed for his hallucinatory potions and retrieved from his medicine bags the talismans he was going to need. He asked the sacred dancers to perform magic steps designed to entrance the Kat-chi-nas, or spirits, to visit the Pueblos.

Only then did the shaman began the rain dance. No one knew when it would end, because it continued until the appearance of black clouds that brought rain to the arid desert soil. The monotonous dance and the insistent chanting tested the stamina of the strongest dancer. After two or three days, the weakest collapsed. New dancers replaced those most worn out, their whole bodies painted with vertical lines symbolizing rain. When at last the Thunderbird groaned, the Pueblos, dripping wet, danced again to thank the rain spirits.

These events could go on for more than two months before the rain arrived – which represented something of a miracle, as in several parts of the desert, one sometimes had to wait two or three years for the rain!

In traditional Indian music, the voice is the most important instrument. There were many kinds of traditional music, ranging from simple short songs to complex song cycles that took days to complete. Besides the voice, musical instruments included drums, rattles, scrapers, and flutes.

A Frenzy of Sound

As is the case with so much of Indian culture, non-natives have had difficulty appreciating Indian music. The sounds produced were often not harmonious. Furthermore, the instruments were often played loudly, with the exception of clay or wood flutes that wooed young women in the Season of Love.

The percussion instruments created the atmosphere and imposed a particular rhythm on each dance. Large drums made of hardened rawhide or of wood covered with a stretched deerskin could not rest on the ground without losing their low-pitched resonance, so some groups suspended them on wooden hooks planted in the ground. They were just as useful for sending messages over long distances as for beating time for the dancers. Their entire decoration consisted of a band of red cloth and feathers.

The musicians emphasized movements of the participants with rattles, called She-she-koi by the Cheyennes, which were made from gourds filled with small pebbles or knucklebones. Around 1750 some people salvaged small bells from the collars of horse harnesses from the Long White Snakes (the wagon trains of the settlers) and tied them to their ankles. Made from the skin of dried fruit, they accompanied the dancers' movements and added to the cacophony of the dances.

The piercing call of the whistle stood out among the sounds of celebration. It contrasted sharply with the repetitive chanting of the chorus.

Noisy meetings, in which each participant told of his own adventures, added to the apparent disorder.

The rawhide calabash filled with small dried fruits made a fine rhythm instrument.

Terracotta or elderwood flutes added a melodious note to the cacophony of chanting.

Rattles made with tiny shakers cut from dried fruit or wild goats' hooves made a rather shrill noise. With the arrival of non-native colonists in the New World, some shakers were gradually replaced with cones cut out of tin cans.

Used to keep the dancer's steps in rhythm, tambourines were made from the skins of wild sheep or deer, stretched over hoops of wood.

On the east and west coasts, sticks were scraped against notched lengths of wood to accompany the dances.

On the path of the warriors

Bow, arrow, tomahawk, and other weapons and tools were essential to Native

American survival. Boys were introduced to handling weapons from early

childhood, and they were raised to be true warriors. The most valiant preferred to die in

combat, rather than pass away in their beds.

Swift and spirited horses were needed for these fearless riders. Mounted warriors practiced actions of combat thousands of times with their animals. Clinging to their manes, hidden behind their flanks and at full gallop, they taught the horses all the stages of an attack.

The Quiver

The quiver, made from untanned leather, was as hard as steel. Plains Indian fighters carried it on their backs in a way that allowed them to grab an arrow over their shoulders with a simple movement. There were hunting arrows and war arrows. The soldiers of the army feared the latter, as they often struck without warning.

Weapons

Indians took great care in making their arrows, as range, penetration, and accuracy depended on the craftsman's skill. Where it was available, the hunter and the warrior chose red cedar by preference, as its dense texture met their needs perfectly. Arrow feathers came, naturally, from birds. Points, previously made from bone or stone, were later cut out of iron barrel hoops. Unwittingly, pioneers supplied a great deal of this material when crossing Indian territory. The tip of a hunting arrow, made in the shape of a willow leaf, could be easily pulled out of an animal and re-used. On the other hand, the war arrow tip was supplied with barbs that prevented its extraction. To remove such an arrow, there was only one option: to push it through so that it emerged opposite its point of entry. An arrow always bore the sign of its owner.

The Bow against the Fire Stick

When some Indian groups acquired horses, they shortened the bow to make it more maneuverable. Men made bows from various woods—Osage orange was a favorite—and made its string from deer and buffalo sinew. Rare whalebone bows were especially prized.

Around 1780, when a Chippewa of the plains was asked which animal was the source of the bone his bow was made from, he replied that it was a medicine wood. In other words, he may not have known. Whales stranded quite frequently on the Pacific coast and their bones occasionally made their way through trade to the Great Plains.

From 1750, the tomahawk became a favorite weapon of some Indians. It was a relatively modern design, derived from those of their ancestors. The weapon consisted of a wooden shaft on the end of which men used rawhide straps to secure a flat stone. Between wars, it could also be used as a tool for splitting wood.

In a hiding place and in a sumptuous container, the shaman kept a special hatchet that was never used for mundane tasks. This miniature reproduction was of purely symbolic importance. Called the war hatchet, it was "dug up" when the shaman or war chief gave the green light to an expedition. The warriors later had to return this emblem, symbol of the Great Spirit's consent to the opening of hostilities.

Dakota men made war shields from the thickest part of a bison's skin: the hump. A defensive weapon par excellence, the shield's manufacture demanded careful preparations. The skin had to be double the size of the finished product. The leather had to be soaked in a paste of boiled hooves mixed with fluid found in the animal's leg joints. The shaven skin steeped for a whole day in this glue, then it was shaped on a heated round stone. In drying, the leather shrank and became hard and tough. All that was left to do was to trim the edges. On the inside, a man fixed the leather band needed to slip over his arm. He decorated the outside with feathers and designs, such as bolts of the Thunder Bird. Thus equipped, the Dakota feared no one. War shields were so tough they were known to deflect even bullets.

THE TOMAHAWK

Some groups possessed a sort of "flying tomahawk" that resembled the boomerang of the Australian Aborigines. It consisted of a flat curved club, made in imitation of the shape of a bird's wing, with the ability to glide and return to the thrower when it missed its target. If the opposite was the case, it was better not to come into contact with the cutting edge of the blade of the murderous tool, otherwise, beast or person would lose his life to it. This swift weapon, in the hands of a skilled hunter, also contributed greatly to the work of feeding the family.

THE SPEAR

Like all weapons and tools, the construction of spears varied widely according to location. Among most Plains groups it measured roughly seven feet in length. It was made of wood, and almost always bore feathers. The blade was shaped according to its use. This lance was most often used for killing bison by piercing straight to the heart.

THE ARROW GAME

Nothing better illustrates the strength of Plains warriors than the Arrow Game. On a given day, competitors assembled on a flat piece of land and took off all unnecessary clothing, retaining only a loincloth. The first pretender to the title of Piercer of Clouds let fly an arrow into the air with all his strength.

Then, so quickly that the eye could not follow his movement, he notched a
second arrow, drew his bow and fired, pulled the string once more and fired
again; more shots followed behind. Judges counted the arrows that flew
through the air together before the first arrow touched the ground. The
number was often as high as ten. The best carried off the title!

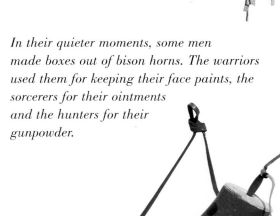

Knives were
often fashioned from
a sabre blade. This one's sheath bears
the mark of the Iroquois League of Six Nations.

Before being a "weapon," the scalping knife was an efficient slicing tool for skinning bison and deer. It was also used for cutting meat in bowls, and for a number of other tasks.

When non-natives arrived, equipped with powder guns, the Indians called the weapons Fire Sticks. At first, the gun was a long flintlock, later replaced by a priming system. The white man carried a powerful medicine with him! Muskets gave way to Sharp, Remington and Winchester rifles. The English exported the Webley, and the French, numerous twelve-shot Lefaucheux revolvers. The Colt, alas, was only a six-shooter. Later came giant cannon and repeating guns, while some Indians still used the bow....

While by at least the early 19th century most Indians were able to trade for significant amounts of guns and cartridges, they were never able to manufacture these weapons.

Depending on the tribe and its circumstances, a gun might be worth the price of a canoe, of several quarters of elk meat, or of a horse. This was why Indians regarded their firearms as precious possessions.

In their quieter moments, some men made boxes out of bison horns. The warriors used them for keeping their face paints, the sorcerers for their ointments and the hunters for their gunpowder.

Coveted Lands

A certain kind of literature and a Hollywood film industry partial to the exotic have shown us a fantasy image of Native Americans. Neither are many school books free of prejudice. Therefore, there are still people for whom Indians are no more than murderous beings – impediments to civilization – who sacrifice their innocent victims at the torture stake. Such images only serve to overheat the imagination and create a barrier to true understanding. The truth is always more complicated than simple representations of good and bad. Some Indians did torture their victims. Some certainly attacked people whom they considered trespassers in violation of sacred treaties and immediate threats to their physical safety, not to mention their way of life. Yet U.S. soldiers just as certainly engaged in massacreing, raping, torturing, and dismembering Indian men, women, and children. The 1864 massacre at Sand Creek, Colorado, was not unique. There, "irregular troops" killed and mutilated hundreds of unarmed Cheyenne and Arapaho Indians, mostly women and children. Black Kettle, the faithful Cheyenne chief, saw his wife fall at his feet, her chest riddled with bullets. There was a kind of irony in this: at the start of the attack, the innocent peaceful families had taken refuge under the star-spangled banner that the Yankees had just given them… as a sign of peace and friendship!

On their arrival in the New World, non-native colonists wished to settle in lands already inhabited by established Indian groups.

A UNITED PEOPLE

Before and even after the arrival of non-natives, many Indian tribes engaged in vicious rivalries. The struggle against the colonists and the U.S. Army, however, sometimes pushed them to try to unite as one people.

Chief Kish-ke-kosh of the Fox tribe.

THE GENERAL AND THE IROQUOIS

When Te-cum-seh, the illustrious Shawnec orator, threatened an American general with mobilizing over six thousand warriors, the furious general retorted that he would have him shot. The Iroquois replied calmly, "Do you believe you can frighten me by talk of harming my body?"

But what did Te-cum-seh mean on that day in 1812? As noted earlier, Native American warriors did not generally fear death; in fact, they welcomed it in the service of bravery, valor and duty.

In the north, the Hurons occupied one of the banks of the Saint Lawrence in a territory that was to become Ontario. To the south, the Iroquois lived in a region the Dutch called New Amsterdam in 1625. Forty years later the English took it and called it New York. The lands to the north became Canada. Whites wanted space and obtained it by force. The already unequal balance of weapons made all the difference.

Non-native intrusions, coupled with the desire of some Northeastern Indians to increase the area of their fur-trapping grounds, led to new conflicts and population movements. The Hurons clashed with the Iroquois. The Ojibwas pushed against the Dakota, who, in turn, leaned on the Cheyennes. The balance was disrupted. Each tribe expanded or abandoned its hunting grounds and encroached on those of its neighbor. The Algonquins named the Dakota the Olla-oke, Foreigners. The Dakota called the Cheyennes Shy-le-as, People of the Strange Tongue. The atmosphere that reigned in the 1750s between the Rocky Mountains in the west and the Mississippi in the east was strained by the groups being forced west by the huge and powerful Ojibwa.

With the introduction of the horse, Great Plains tribes increasingly developed a horse-based culture that revolved around bison, hunting and warfare/raiding. Military societies began to assume growing importance. Some acted as camp police. Some were responsible for keeping order on the hunt. Some, such as the Dog Soldiers, were considered the bravest of the brave. Groups like this sometimes adopted apparently bizarre behaviors, like acting or speaking in opposites.

At first this could seem unlikely. But, examining Indian feelings, there was nothing abnormal about this development. In the context of a warrior culture, the Dog Soldier defended his people with faith and passion. Fathers had the task of teaching sons to become valiant warriors: bringing out the fighting spirit of each young man in this way was the price that had to be paid for the survival of these people. The young child learned to handle weapons before he could put on his moccasins. Little interested the Dog Soldier beyond the art of fighting, and to let the other members of the tribe understand this, the members of this society did everything backward to accentuate the contrast. The Contrary Dog displayed his disdain for and detachment from everyday tasks, sleeping in the day and being active at night. If he had to attend the council, he sat in the circle of elders, but covered his head with a blanket, showing that his body was present but his mind was elsewhere… on the paths of war!

Despite the uneasiness that his behavior aroused among the people, the man was wholeheartedly respected: they knew that during the next fight, he would return to his normal behavior, planting his spear in the ground and never retreating. His Dog Warrior's club in his hand, he would fight to the death.

As part of the warrior culture, Plains Indians created the system of war honors called counting coup. Various acts of bravery were ranked according to their relative difficulty.

To kill an enemy known for his bravery was good, but to return with this man's tomahawk or war-club without injuring him was more courageous. Had the victorious fighter not doubled the danger? By allowing his adversary to live, he risked being determinedly pursued by the offended warrior!

A fighter achieved great fame if a witness could confirm that he had struck his rival only once. A supreme exploit was to return with an enemy's medicine bag. By doing this, paradoxically, one killed him twice by letting him live: the dispossessed man would be rejected by his people who would consider him dead, and he regarded himself as being reduced to the status of a corpse. He found himself defenseless in the face of the evil spirits and could only bring bad luck to his people.

In 1845, George Catlin painted Little Wolf, the famous Cheyenne warrior. After his tribe was deported to a reservation in Oklahoma, he decided to lead his people toward their homeland in the north. Accompanied by Dull Knife and 300 others, he was one of the heroes of the 1878 Long March of the Cheyennes.

The Dog Warrior

After 1880, a rumor went around that the Plains Indians had only been able to win the great battle of the Little Bighorn by a radical change of strategy. For the first time they had seen fit to waive their principles and dismount from their horses in order to fight.

After the acquisition of the horse, Plains Indians believed that they owed their successes to their mounts. The animal's noble spirit and its courage in battle made it an ally from which the Indian could not bear to be parted, even in peacetime! Confident in their opinion, several Dog Warriors decided to mount their animals and never dismount. By this action they made it known that they devoted themselves to war and that nothing else counted for them. The fact that a man behaved in this way brought little inconvenience to the village. But when one examines the consequences of such a decision, one wonders how a society can adjust to such a situation.

To show the others more clearly his total disdain for mundane

Certain warriors had the heavy responsibility of keeping watch on every movement of their enemies. At the top of a mountain, hidden behind a rock, a scout stayed on the lookout for hours at a time. His eyes gazed on the fort, convoys, and troop movements. The survival of the entire people might rest with this one man. At his signal, the Dog Soldiers launched their lightning attack.

activities, the Dog Warrior asked his women to embroider sacred symbols on the soles of his moccasins: thus attired he could no longer place his feet on the ground without offending the spirits.

Seated from dawn to dusk on horseback, the Dog Warrior had his meals brought to him there, and if the women did not arrive on time, they were brought into line very effectively: "Are these women going to allow that man to die of hunger and thirst? Don't they see how much he suffers from this situation brought about by this time of peace?" The Dog Warrior did not expect to have any part of a "normal" life, and everyone was careful to avoid saying a word on this subject. Freedom of thought and of action was paramount, and no one dared complain about problems caused by the Dog Warrior.

Today, it seems difficult to explain how this man rested. Perhaps he slept on his horse, or maybe his women kept silent and turned a blind eye when he slipped into the tepee.

THE CONTRARY DOGS

The experience of Ee-a-chi-che-a, or Red Thunder, is typical. Hardly out of his cradle, Red Thunder, the little Cheyenne, took an interest in weapons. His father, Black Moccasins, taught him to make a bow and arrows. After a few snows, he declared that Red Thunder would become a good warrior. He took part in his father's horse-stealing raids. But one day, an Osage killed Black Moccasins and stole his medicine bag. Red Thunder vowed to win back his father's honor.

One night, the Cheyenne sneaked into the tepee of his Osage enemy, Fast Man. He satisfied his hunger by smoking the Osage's tobacco before killing him, and then recovered the medicine bag. After this victory, on his return to his camp, Red Thunder took the name He Who Kills the Osages. But soon, dreams and visions crept over him. One of these visions oriented him toward a new way of living. One morning, an elder saw him rolling in the dust, jumping into the river and watering his horse. Seeing this, the old man put his hand over his mouth. The morning purification ritual followed an unchanging routine: the Indian watered his horse, then he washed himself and dried himself by rolling on the ground. Having done all this backward, He Who Kills the Osages moved away, riding his horse facing its rump. He Who Kills the Osages had become a Contrary Dog!

Then one morning, he emerged from his tepee with his body painted for war. In one hand he held his war spear. In the other, a curved stick decorated with eagle feathers, ermine, and otter skin. He brandished it and cried out, "Here is the Staff of the Contrary Dogs! Its medicine is so strong that when they see it the enemies of the Human Beings will be struck down. Before the snow returns there will be scalps handing from it. No arrow will harm my chest for it is like a rock, and the bear would break its claws on it. The Creator has placed lightning bolts in my hands and they will strike through our enemies. Those who follow me will be invulnerable and victorious. I have spoken and it is good. How!"

In a dignified silence, the people withdrew to discuss the event. By his tirade, the Cheyenne had just lost all his former names. Now everyone knew him as a Contrary Dog: Shon-ka, The Dog!

The Scalp

Taking scalps was not an Indian invention. We should not forget that in 445, Attila, King of the Huns, presented himself to the Gauls with scalps hanging from his belt and from his horse's bridle. In Canada, the French and English revived the practice to exercise some control over the murderous activities of their allies, the Hurons and the Iroquois. Rewards were plentiful: a cotton blanket for one scalp, a wooden-handled knife for two scalps.

Most Indians did not consider taking scalp to be a gratuitous act of cruelty. Warriors took part in the practice for a very precise reason. Some believed that at birth the Great Spirit lent him a body that he had to return intact after his death. To return even a partially

In the sixteenth century, painters represented Indians as savage and bloodthirsty beings who scalped their fellows alive.

At the end of the seventeenth century, the same "savages" still took scalps, but this time from the dead. A change of interpretation...

incomplete set of mortal remains was taking a risk of being denied entry to the after life, and of seeing oneself driven away into the Land of Shadows. Now, one's enemy is by nature an odious being whom no one would like to meet in an idyllic place. Logic demanded that one deprive one's enemy of part of his anatomy so that, after he died, he would inhabit a place where there was no longer any risk of bumping into him. This belief was so deeply rooted that sometimes an Indian even mutilated himself. For example, if he lost a loved one and found himself grief stricken, he might deny himself entry to the after life by cutting off a finger so that the other souls in paradise would not have to endure his great sorrow.

Indians rarely scalped living enemies, but sometimes people who had lost consciousness and been left for dead woke up too late. In any case, the scalper never made contact with the bone: after the wound had healed, a round bald patch was left on the top of the head. Perhaps the habit, in the West, of always keeping a hat clamped onto one's head was started by some scalped non-natives.

After the customary ceremonies and the Dance of Forgiveness, the scalp could be used to decorate the entrance to a tepee or the bridle of a horse. Next to a warrior's funeral scaffold, it indicated the tomb of a warrior. Locks of scalp adorned feather headdresses and clothing.

THE SCALP DANCE

Depending on the tribe, the Scalp Dance, or the Dance of Forgiveness, took place at night at the end of great battles. Inspired by a legend in which the Great Spirit refused entry to the after life to the Silent Warrior (that is, to one who presented himself without the full complement of attributes that the Eternal Being had lent to him at birth), the Dance of Forgiveness consisted of apologizing to the victims for having taken their scalps.

The warriors who took part in the battle re-enacted it in a mournful dance, full of sorrow. Half naked or dressed in rags, and armed with their tomahawks, they brandished poles on the end of which hung the scalps taken from their enemies. And as the drums beat wildly, the victorious warriors pounded the earth to the sound of lamentations. Their faces became horrible. The warriors showed their teeth in frightful grimaces, their nostrils quivering. They competed to look the most terrifying. When this parody of battle was over, each Indian scratched at the ground, pretending to bury his scalp or scalps, then stood up and begged the forgiveness of his enemies, until the sorcerer cut short the lamentations by announcing that he had been communing with the spirits. Wanting to sound convincing, he stated that the latter had agreed to make an exception and admit the defeated enemies into his paradise. The dance ended and everyone went to decorate his clothes, his weapons and the bridle of his horse with the scalps he had so brutally acquired.

The publisher would like to thank the following for their valuable co-operation :

Marguerite Parquet

Héläne Foisil, librarian at the Musée de L'Homme, Paris

Corinne Messager, of Agence Artephot

Denis Mignon-Godefroy

Olivier Balanqueux

Jean-Loup Charmet

Yac

and all the men and "win" who allowed Willian Camus

to retell the lives of their ancestors.

Table of Contents

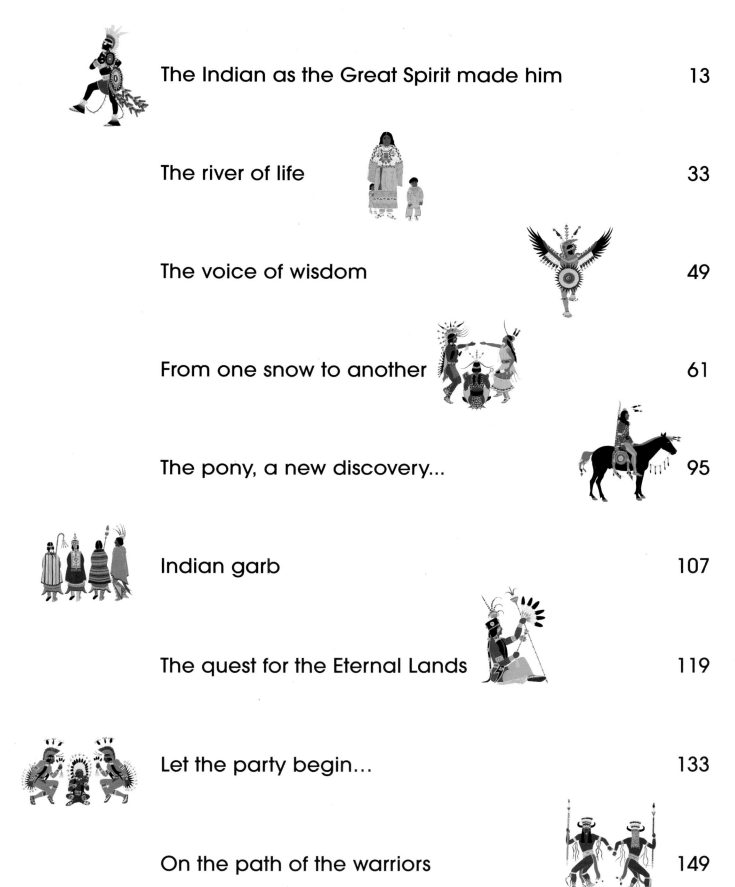

Photographic references

This work was produced by Partenaires in June 1997.